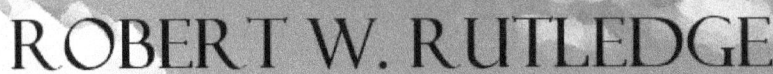

ROBERT W. RUTLEDGE

The Rooming House

*CREATE CASH FLOW
& BUILD YOUR WEALTH
WITH REAL ESTATE,
NO MATTER THE ECONOMY*

THE ROOMING HOUSE
Create Cash Flow And Build Your Wealth With Real Estate, No Matter The Economy
Robert W. Rutledge

Published by Maple Hills Press
Copyright © 2012 by Rutledge Publishing, LLC
All Rights Reserved

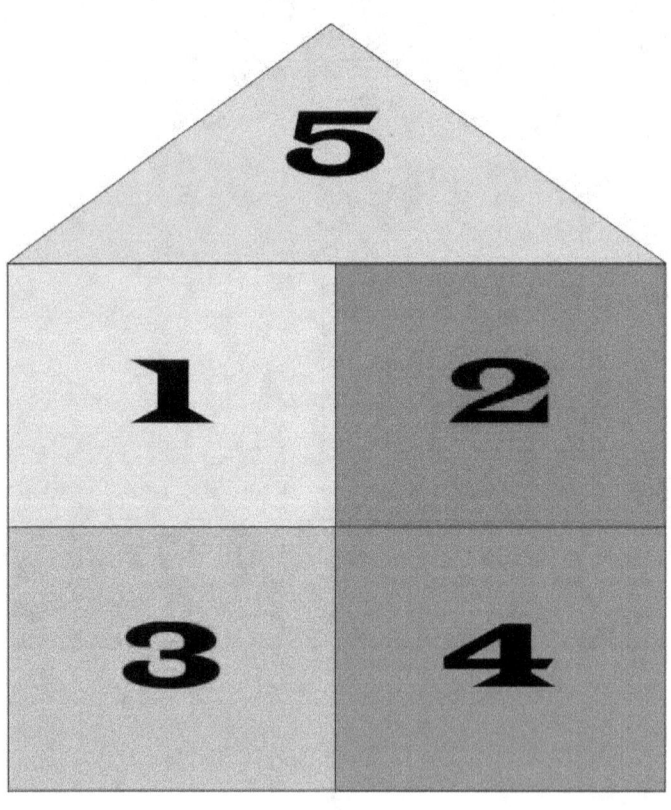

OVERVIEW

One of the biggest mistakes people make when investing in single family houses is thinking that renting out the entire property and getting only $100 – $200 a month in cash flow is a good thing. What if I told you that you could do much better? Would you get into the business if you could make $1,000 a month or more, *after* expenses, on each property? Why settle for only a couple of hundred dollars when you can make five- to ten-times that amount every month? Now do that a few more times to *really* impact your lifestyle! I've done it and so can you!

This book is about purchasing single-family homes and turning them into rooming houses. By renting individual rooms to different people, rather than renting the entire home to a single person or family, you increase your cash flow significantly.

So many books on real estate investing do not get into the nuts and bolts of how to duplicate what the author said was possible. I want to get right down to it so that anyone reading this book can see what to do, what not to do, and what *I've* done to acquire properties with good, positive cash-flow potential.

I share with you the finer details of what to look for in properties, how to manage them, and why this is a very profitable niche—a niche that is often overlooked by most real-estate investors.

If you have an interest in real estate, but are concerned about the risks; if you can use more monthly cash flow, this system may be for you. This is not a get-rich-quick scheme. This is long-term investing.

My Thanks

My thanks go to my very good friend Christy Kurth, my realtor and fellow investor, whom from the beginning believed in me, supported my goals, and encouraged my dreams. You went above and beyond what a realtor typically does for her clients and have since become an essential business consultant and valued friend.

Special thanks go to my mom and dad who gave me the support I needed and believed in me enough to get me started in real estate with my very first investing book so many years ago; their dedication and positive spirit have always been something I know I can lean on and turn to for guidance. Unfailingly, you were there. You have shown me what it truly means to be a contributing member of society, a proper business owner, and most importantly, a good parent.

My utmost thanks and love go to my family. My wonderful wife, Tiwi, and my children, Aldi and Jaslyn, who all know how passionate I am about this type of real estate investing and who have grown with me on this journey we have undertaken together.

Dedication

This book is dedicated to my very good friend, Larry Mon. It was your willingness to share and to teach that gave me the resolve to follow in your footsteps and use your model as my own. I have tweaked it, modified it, and hopefully have improved upon it.

Without your inspiration, I wouldn't be in this business. You were first my landlord, my role model, my mentor, and then most importantly, my very dear friend. Larry, wherever you are now, I hope I have made you proud. Your laughter is definitely missed.

In Memory of

This book is in memory of my mother, Susann Rutledge. My mother never gave up on anything; she always believed that whatever she put her mind to, she could and would accomplish. A son could never ask for a more wonderful person to have as part of his foundation in life. I am most fortunate to have had her in my life for as long as she was. Mom gave me the base upon which to build everything and with all my love, I thank you!

TABLE OF CONTENTS

Chapter 01 – *Rooms To Rent? Rooming House? What's That?*
Chapter 02 – *Is This Idea A Good Investment?*
Chapter 03 – *House A vs. House B*
Chapter 04 – *Maximizing The Property's Potential*
Chapter 05 – *Recession Proof?*
Chapter 06 – *Keep Your Day Job*
Chapter 07 – *Can It Work In Your Primary Residence?*
Chapter 08 – *Combining Households, A Real-World Example*
Chapter 09 – *Combining Households, Another Real-World Example*
Chapter 10 – *Why This Might Not Be For Me*
Chapter 11 – *What To Do First*
Chapter 12 – *What To Do Second*
Chapter 13 – *What Next?*
Chapter 14 – *Picking The Right Property*
Chapter 15 – *Making An Offer*
Chapter 16 – *Property Inspection*
Chapter 17 – *Closing*
Chapter 18 – *Suggestions For Preparing The House For Tenants*
Chapter 19 – *How To Advertise And Attract Tenants?*
Chapter 20 – *Funding*
Chapter 21 – *Tenants*
Chapter 22 – *Management Do's And Don'ts*
Chapter 23 – *Maintenance*
Chapter 24 – *Appliance Repair*
Chapter 25 – *Unannounced Visits*
Chapter 26 – *Lawn Care / Snow Removal*
Chapter 27 – *Pets*
Chapter 28 – *Insects & Other Pests*
Chapter 29 – *Children And Other Guests*
Chapter 30 – *Cable & Internet*
Chapter 31 – *Bookkeeping*
Chapter 32 – *Washers/Dryers*
Chapter 33 – *Vending Machines*
Chapter 34 – *Ice-Dams And Their Removal*
Chapter 35 – *Collecting Rent*
Chapter 36 – *Insurance*
Chapter 37 – *Incorporating?*

Chapter 38 – *What Happens After You've Purchased Your 4th Property And Want to Purchase More*
Chapter 39 – *Designated As "Primary Residence"*
Chapter 40 – *Other Benefits*
Chapter 41 – *Exit Strategy*

Appendix A – Copy Of Lease
Appendix B – Property Information
Appendix C – Eviction Notice
Appendix D – Reminder
Appendix E – Rent Drawer
Appendix F – Thermostat Settings
Appendix G – Duct Cleaning
Appendix H – Front Door Lock Change
Appendix I – Carpet Cleaning
Appendix J – De-bugging House

About The Author

CHAPTER 1
Rooms To Rent? Rooming House? What's That?

This is not a new concept. Renting rooms in one's house or home or business has been around forever. It is called many things in many places: *rooms to let, rooms to rent, shared housing, rooming houses, the bunk in back,* etc. Some people mistakenly refer to this as being similar to *college dorms,* which it is not. The only similarity is that there are many people living together under the same roof, but it is different as everyone has their own room and it's not a *party* atmosphere. It is like having your own home within a home. It is an essential housing service which works well in a professional format.

It has been called many things, but the concept has always been the same: people provide a place to sleep or *stay* in their home or building for someone passing through or coming to stay in that area for a period of time. The period of time ranges from days to years, depending on what the owner is offering and what the tenant needs. That person or *tenant* would, in turn, usually provide something of value in return for safe lodging. As time has gone on it has become a more common thing to pay cash rather than to exchange services; but there are exceptions, as even to this day, people barter for things and renting rooms is no exception.

Today's rooming houses offer people a clean, habitable, and safe environment. Utilities may be included. Weekly, monthly, or other periodic terms may be offered as well. Flexibility and versatility are key features of this business.

CHAPTER 2
Is This Idea A Good Investment?

A good place to start

You may say to yourself, "I want to invest in multi-family units someday, but I want to start out small and gain expertise. I can learn from my mistakes with smaller investments and then work my way up; that way, my mistakes will be smaller and therefore will have less of an impact on my bottom line; then I can use the knowledge I've gained and start purchasing larger buildings with more units."

Why?

Not everyone can get started investing in multi-family dwellings or other types of real estate right away; and not everyone wants to purchase a single family property if it's only going to generate $100-$200 per month in profit. If one major appliance breaks, you're out most of your cash flow for the entire year; if your one tenant can't pay, or moves out and trashes your property, again your cash flow is greatly reduced.

Still other people do not want the headaches of purchasing a single family property and renting it to only one person or family when there is little control over that property once it's rented. In most states, when a property is rented to one person or one family, the landlord may be required to give at least 24 hours' notice to enter the property. Usually you can only inspect the property once a year. The point is that these time lapses can result in properties suffering extensive damage without your knowledge.

I know of far too many stories with properties rented this way. It usually goes something like this:

Everything seemed fine for most of the year until the tenant started falling behind on paying the rent. The landlord is willing to work with the tenant at this point; then it gets worse and either the landlord's phone calls go unreturned or the people just move out. More than likely, they leave behind a mess for the landlord to clean up. Hopefully, he's required and received enough of a damage deposit to cover his repairs, but that is rare. It is very easy for the repairs to exceed the deposit amount collected. Once the tenant has vacated the property, the repairs begin; this puts the entire property off the rental market for weeks at a time—perhaps months, depending on what damage was done to the property. Now, not only has the landlord lost the income from the previous tenant, he has to make repairs from the damage deposit; and now the property sits vacant for days or weeks, losing even more money. All for just $100 – $200 per month in cash flow, if he's lucky.

Does this sound like a good way to make money fast? If you're like me, then no, it doesn't sound like a great way to make money in real estate—not when there's a better way.

Positive, lucrative, cash-flowing rooming houses work differently. In properties that are set up to be rooming houses, the tenants are less likely to damage the property completely since there are other tenants living on the same property. Tenants usually do not take out their frustrations on the other tenants; their frustrations are usually intended for the landlord. When renting a single room, a tenant has less space available in the house to do intentional damage; they do not have access to the other tenants' rooms; and in many situations, frustrated tenants do not want witnesses to their destruction. In all my years of managing and owning rooming houses, I have never had an entire house destroyed or vandalized by current or former tenants. These destructive and problem tenants will usually only make a mess of their own room while leaving the rest of the house intact. Renting out an entire house invites much more extensive damage. You can easily go in, make the repairs, and clean up the destruction that was left behind, all while not disturbing your other tenants; therefore, your investment is still producing good cash flow.

A rooming house can help you do that. Rooming houses are a great way to get into the game of real estate investing—and as you add to your portfolio, they will allow you to move up to larger investments if that is your choice. A rooming house can also be a great way to supplement your income if you're looking for just a little more money to bring home every month. If you only want to have one investment property, then one can work for you; if you want to have many more houses in your portfolio, then this plan can work for you as well.

You might be saying to yourself, "Well that's fine, but why a rooming house? Isn't that more work and more headaches than just renting out a single family house to one renter or one family?"

Well, frankly no. Depending on how well you manage your property, it can be very little work and hardly any headaches at all. If, given a choice between a single family house that cash flows over $500 – $1000 per month requiring a little more management, or a single family house that cash flows about $100 – $200 per month with very little management, which would you rather have? If you're like me, you'd rather have the property that cash flows the most, even if it took a little bit more of your time. If you can make $500 – $1000 per month or more on one property, wouldn't you want to do it again as soon as you could? You bet you would! Once I saw how it worked, I repeated it again and again.

Now, if you do not manage it properly, then yes, it can be much more time consuming. You could still cash flow well, but it will eat up more of your time and money. I've found this to be true. This has happened to me. However, as time goes on, you will gain experience and knowledge which will help you avoid such calamities, keeping headaches at a minimum, and profits at a maximum. With this book, *The Rooming House*, you'll be able to see many of the problems I've run into and the solutions I've used over the years while engaged in the business of managing rooming houses.

CHAPTER 3
House A vs. House B

Here's a real-world example:

Figure 1

There are two houses next to each other that are exactly alike; we will call them House A and House B. They both are four-bedroom, two-bath houses, with two-car detached garages in a typical suburban neighborhood. See the example above in Fig. 1

House A, at the time it was purchased, was rented to one family at $1,200 per month. The 30-year fixed-rate mortgage payment is $1,065 per month including property tax and property insurance. The tenant pays all the utilities; they take care of the house and the yard upkeep. Simple cash flow is $1,200 − $1,065 = $135 per month.

House A

Monthly Rent	$1,200
Mortgage (if any)	- $1,065
Subtotal	$135
Utilities	- $0
TOTAL CASH FLOW	$135

That's if nothing breaks or needs to be repaired. If something breaks, who pays for it? That's right, just because a tenant was using the dishwasher, doesn't mean that the tenant has to pay for it. You, the landlord, will probably have to have it replaced. A decent, basic, dishwasher can run $400. There goes your cash flow for three months ($135 x 3 months = $405).

House B was rented to four separate individual tenants for a total of $1,800 per month—or $450 per tenant, multiplied by 4 tenants = $1,800. The utilities are paid by the landlord.

The utilities average per month:

Utilities

Cable (optional)	$100
Water/Sewer	$40
Electric	$100
Gas	$80
Garbage	$35
TOTAL	$355

So now it looks like this:

House B	
Monthly Rents	$1,800
Mortgage (if any)	-$1,065
Subtotal	$735
Utilities	- $355
TOTAL CASH FLOW	$380

That's $380 in cash flow per month!

You have now just increased your cash flow by $245 per month (House B's cash flow $380 – House A's cash flow $135 = $245). This is an 81% pay raise for yourself, without doing anything differently, other than renting to more tenants! Doesn't this give you more leeway when it comes to repairs? Yes, it does.

Now, let's look at it more closely. Let's say two tenants in House B want to use the garage to park their cars to keep the snow and ice off of them in the winter. Do they get the use of the garage for free? No, they do not! So you rent out each stall to the tenants for $25 each, per month. Now you've increased your cash flow another $50 per month!!

Looking at it again, you know that the bedrooms aren't the same size. Some are much bigger and one even has its own bathroom. Can you get more for a room that is larger or has its own bathroom than you can for rooms of comparable size or with no bathroom? Sure you can. Renters all want their own bathrooms. If the base rent each month is $450 per month, larger rooms can easily be $25 – $100 more a month, especially if they have their own bathroom. So for this example of House B, one of the bedrooms is a master bedroom, and of the three remaining bedrooms, one is bigger than the other two but smaller than the master. Since the other room is bigger, you can get $475 for it—an increase of $25 per month. The master bedroom often commands an additional $100 for it since it has its own bathroom. This will vary by the area in which your property is located.

You have now just increased the amount of rent you're getting each month by $175 ($100 for the master bedroom with a private bathroom, plus $25 for the larger room, and plus $50 for two garage stalls) by doing nothing else, other than looking at what is already part of the property. The total cash flow for the property is now the starting amount of $380 plus $175, for a total of $555!! How long would it take to pay for a new $400 dishwasher now? That impacts your cash flow dramatically!!

CHAPTER 4
Maximizing The Property's Potential

Whenever I look for property that would work for my business, I always think about what other potential that property holds. What I mean by that is what else I can do with the property that someone else hasn't thought of before. What ways can I get it to generate more income for me with the least expense?

Here's the real secret of having rooming houses in your portfolio. What if you took that same property, House B, as used in Chapter 3, but maximized the cash flow even more? How do you do this? One way is to look at the total square feet of the property and its interior layout and see how it can be maximized. For House B, I noticed this property had a lot of wasted space in the basement that wasn't being utilized to its full potential. With a small investment of time, skill, and labor by me and my family, we were able to change the layout of the basement from only one legal bedroom to three, using the same square footage. (See Fig. 2)

Early that next year I started to do minor renovations—upgrading and improving the property by modifying the lower level. It was originally just a living room, a bathroom, a double bedroom, and a laundry/utility room; without changing the square footage, I modified it to be three legal bedrooms by installing two legal-size egress windows, egress window pits, and separating the double bedroom into two legal bedrooms. (If you do not know already, an egress window is a window that is large enough for a firefighter to fit into with an air tank on his back when the bedroom is partially or completely below ground level. Check the code of the city you are purchasing in to make sure your window size is up to code.) I then modified the laundry/utility room and maximized the space and put the third bedroom in that location.

Remodeling can be a lot of hard work if you do it yourself, but well worth the expense, time, and effort in the long run. Those two additional rooms still bring in an additional $900 per month! That's each and every month for the last 13 years! If you were to pay someone else to install the windows, it would cost you about $1,000 per egress window, so you'd still recoup the cost within a few months; but I did the work myself and recouped that cost even faster, minus the blood and sweat. (I've gained another skill and now know how to do it myself.)

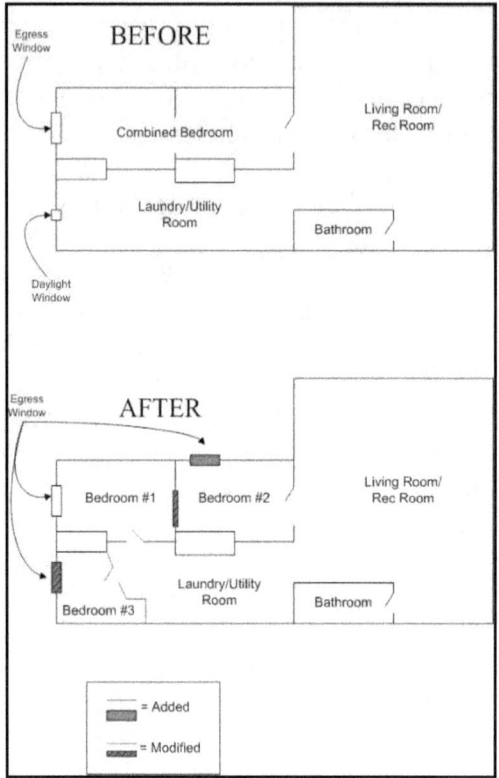

Figure 2

Now, instead of only having one bedroom at $450 to rent out in the basement, I now had three. At just the $450 minimum amount for each additional bedroom I had increased my cash flow by $900 per month for as long as I own the property!! Let me say it again, I increased my cash flow by $900 per month for as long as I own the property!!

That was over 13 years ago and I still own the property today. The initial expense of those additional rooms paid for themselves many times over.

Adding the cash flow amount of $555 from Chapter 2, plus $900 for the two rooms I added, the cash flow is now $1,455 per month!!! You should use the 10% vacancy factor when figuring cash flow in real estate, but now figure 10% on being just one empty room, which does happen from time to time. Now the net cash flow is at $1,005. Chump change? I think not. Again, do this three, four times and you're looking at probably enough to match your salary from your day job.

So, the total cash flow for this house:

Rents (6 bedrooms)	$2,875
Mortgage	- $1,065
Subtotal	$1,810
Utilities/Expenses	- $355
TOTAL CASH FLOW	$1,455

My mortgage payment, including hazard insurance and property taxes, was $1,065 on a 30-year fixed mortgage rate of 6.5 percent. Since I was living in the master bedroom ($475) and renting out the other five bedrooms, my total rental income was lower, at a combined $2,400 per month. My expenses for the property, including utilities, were $355 per month. My cash flow was then $905 per month!!! So, $2,400 – $1,065 – $355 = $980. Not a $1,000, you say? True, but I'm also living there rent free!!! That's saving me at least an additional $475 a month in rent I don't have to pay to someone else.

At $2,400 in rent a month, multiplied by 12 months = $28,800 per year. $28,800 divided by my down payment of $5,000 = a 576% return on my investment, or cash on cash return (COCR) in the first year!!! Of course that's gross return on my investment. The net return on my investment after mortgage payments and utility expenses is the following: $28,800 gross rents – mortgage payments

$12,780 – utilities $4,260 = $11,760. Figuring in 10% for vacancy, my net return is $10,584. So, my rough net for the year was only $10,584 and my down payment was $5,000. I just doubled my money in one year and you can do this too!! Or to be more exact, I had a 212% COCR on my net investment!!! Not bad for the first year. And the best part was that I was living at the property for free and my tenants were paying me to live there!!

Now if I would have been renting out the master instead of living in it, what would my return on the investment be? Even at $475 per month, I saved myself from having to pay rent of $5,700 per year. That's money going straight into my pocket.

If you did this once, do you think you'd want to do it again and then again? You bet you would!!!! As did I.

There are many other ways to maximize a property's potential. For example, the second house I bought was in a different suburb, in a nice neighborhood; but the property was beginning to look a little run down. It definitely wasn't the nicest property on the block, but I could see its potential. It was a 3,500 sq. ft. single-family house with five bedrooms and a lower-level family room that was being used as a sixth bedroom. It had an extra-wide driveway and the best part of it, not only its size and number of bedrooms, was the fact that it had two entrances on the front of the house—one for the upper level of the house and one for the walkout basement, both on the front of the house!! (See Fig. 3 below.) As an option for the future, I knew immediately that I could eventually separate this house into a duplex. I bought it and starting fixing it up even as I rented it out.

BEFORE

AFTER

Figure 3

The beauty of purchasing rental property for this purpose is that you can start renting out rooms immediately, even if the rest of the property needs to be improved. As long as it's habitable and up to code, you can rent it out. I have made many improvements and repairs to a property while the tenants were living there. I haven't had vacancies while I'm working on another room. This is usually not the case when you are renting out the entire property to someone; they want and rightly expect the entire house to be completed before they move in, costing you time and money.

Figure 4

My next property met all of my criteria and still had room to expand. It was a four-bedroom house with room in the basement to add two more bedrooms without much work (See Fig. 4). I quickly did the modifications and rented the additional rooms for an increase in income of $900 per month. I was cash flowing on this property over $1,500 per month. The best part about this property's potential was almost an acre of undeveloped land just off a busy intersection; the other three corners of this intersection are commercialized and it is only a matter of time before I would be approved to sell for commercial use. There isn't much undeveloped land left this close to the highway and my property had the only highway access to this extra corner's land. Even if this property never becomes commercial, I can still subdivide it and develop a few small apartment buildings or more single-family homes. The property has great potential and I have many options. Today many years later this property is still one of my best purchases. Again, recognizing and maximizing a property's potential.

How about external storage? Many times people overlook what they have available to them on their very own property or a property they're investing in. Is the property accessible from other sides? Meaning does it have streets that run along it, alleyways, etc. If it does, then it's easily accessible for storage for boats, RVs, campers, etc. With an easily-accessible property that's large enough to accommodate a number of vehicles, you could easily add positive cash flow to your bottom line. I've had tenants store boats and RVs on my property while they're renting with me for an additional $25/mo. per vehicle. If you had room for four vehicles, there's an additional $100/mo. in pure positive cash flow. The best part is that the people who rent out space from you don't have to be tenants, either!

Be sure to do your due diligence on this since you could run up against zoning ordinances with the city or town you're investing in that may or may not limit how they are to be stored (i.e. tires must be on some harder surface, such as blocks or asphalt, etc.), how many can be on the property at the same time, etc. You may also have to screen them from the street and your neighbors' property as well. Some people won't appreciate looking into their backyard and having to see a 25-foot RV parked right up against their fence every day. You may also want to check with your insurance company, as well.

So you see, from some of my examples, it's not only what you immediately notice when you look at a property, it's what other potential the property has that could be the real bread and butter for you.

CHAPTER 5
Recession Proof?

Owning rooming houses are about as recession proof as it gets in the world of real estate investing. When you think in terms of housing and what happens during a recession, people for whatever reason have to downsize their lifestyle. This has happened over and over again in history and even after we are well beyond this current recession, it will happen again someday down the road. People downsize for a variety of reasons—often they need to save money and they can't afford their current housing expense. They do it not only with their housing, but with all parts of their life. For example, instead of eating at their favorite restaurant, they'll switch to eating fast food; they might even eat out less all together and instead prepare more food at home and *brown-bag* it to work. These same people might choose to forgo the movie theater at $12+ a person in favor of watching TV at home, watching movies on the internet, or even browsing $1 rental kiosks at the local convenience store. When the economy stalls or turns downward, people will find ways to cut corners, which also applies to their housing.

Housing is one of the greatest expenses of a person's budget every month. If you can cut that in half or by a third for them, that's significant. People who go from paying $800 per month, plus utilities, for an apartment, are more than willing to pay $450 for a place that *includes* utilities, even if it means sharing some common living areas with others. That's where rooming houses make great investments—and even more so during a recession, since they provide a much-needed, affordable alternative.

Uncontrollable market conditions

I have been investing in rooming houses since 1998. Back then, interest rates had just dropped to an all-time low of 6.5% for a 30-year fixed mortgage. At that time, it was the lowest rates had ever been. People were making a mad dash for the stock market, which was beginning to take off. Real estate was just starting its upward trend that has lasted until just recently. During the stock market boom years, this business prospered.

In August of 2001, I had just closed on another property and was starting to get it leased up. When 9/11 happened, everything came to a halt. If you remember, people were hesitant about just about everything; but it wasn't long after that that people began moving again, and very quickly my new rooming house was completely full. To this very day, that property is almost always full. Even during the worst terrorist attack our country has seen to date, this business prospered.

My rooming house business made it through the early days of the stock market craziness in the late '90s, the tragedy of 9/11, the housing boom of the early 2000s, and now the current housing and financial bust. In 2007 and 2008, as job losses mounted and more and more people lost their homes to subprime mortgages, my rooming houses filled up even faster and have stayed full.

Filling a need

In times like these, it comes back to the basics. People have to eat and they need someplace to live. People have to live somewhere. Many of them will find places to stay—with friends or relatives—while some become homeless and others manage to find an apartment to lease. But there is still a large group of people who either can't afford an apartment because money is tight or their rental and credit history presents barriers; they may have stayed with family and friends for a while, but after some time had to move on. When times are tough, rooming houses provide a valued, under-recognized service to each and every community.

Also, how about people who have just moved into the area for a job relocation or are going to school? People who are going to college and want something less expensive and not as noisy as a dorm; or people who are retirees living on a fixed income. Many of my renters, past and present, are people who are going back to school to improve their situation and who have *been there and done that* when it comes to living in dorms. Dorms do not fit their current lifestyle and this is definitely not a dorm.

As you can see, this business can serve many different clients. I've had everyone from high school students to grandparents renting rooms from me over the years—and some tenants have been renting from me for over 10 years!

There are not many types of real estate that you can get into with as little effort. This type of housing fills a need and provides consistent income, year after year, no matter the economic environment our country is in. This is it! This concept could be the key to your financial success!!

When you think about what is happening now, people are losing their homes, their jobs, and everything else in between. This business is still prospering; it provides a needed, vital service to any community—a service that will reward you handsomely.

CHAPTER 6
Keep Your Day Job

I recommend that you begin small and treat this as a part-time business. You can easily do this on the side while you're working full time. If you so choose, in time you can scale this concept up enough to phase out of your job and have this business sustain you for as long as you wish. I do not recommend quitting your day job right away, unless you have other resources in place to augment your income until such time as the business gets up to scale and can sufficiently replace not only the income from your job but the employment benefits you will need to replace as well. Remember, it's not just about replacing your income from your job, but also the benefits you get by having that job (medical, dental, 401K, etc.). I recommend starting small to make sure that you've picked the best area after reading this book and that there is enough of a demand for this type of business in the city/town you live in or are investing in.

By starting small and keeping your job, you'll also know if this is a passion for you.

CHAPTER 7
Can It Work In Your Primary Residence?

That depends. If you live in a condo, apartment, or townhome, it would depend on the rules and regulations of the complex you live in. Do you own it or do you rent it? Obviously if you rent it, it makes it that much harder, since you have to abide by someone else's rules; if you own your home, it would depend on the layout and the number of available bedrooms and the other rules in place, such as the neighborhood/building's association's rules, if any, and the city and county codes, if any.

For my business, I have found it to be much easier and simpler than multi-family to use single family properties and turn them into rooming houses. But you can rent out a room or two in your apartment, condo or townhome without too much hassle in most places. I have lived in many of these and people all over the world continue to do this, to either help reduce their rent or to help them afford a better place to live. It is very common. Just be sure to check with the rules and regulations of the property you're living in or investing in before you proceed down this path.

If your primary residence is a single family home and you do not mind renting it out to others, it can make a significant difference to your bottom line. See the example "House B" again in Chapter 3.

You might be saying to yourself, "Well, that would mean that I'd have to have other people in my house, using my things, and I'd have to be more careful about walking around naked in my house."

Well, yes.

But if that is something you're not willing to do, then this idea of renting out part of your primary residence is not for you. Do not worry: using your own home is not for everyone. You can still own and manage rooming houses.

But if you are willing to rent out your primary residence and you do not mind sharing the common areas of your residence, it can significantly impact your bottom line! It just depends on what your own personal goals are and what you're willing to do to reach them.

My Family?

Or you might be saying, "My family and I really want to do this, and that may work well for a single person, but what about my family?"

My response to that is if you're trying to save some money, then take a good look at what you can do with the property. Can you and your family live in just the upstairs (or the downstairs, depending on its layout) of your house and then rent out the remaining part of your home? Can it be split into a duplex type of house where there is more than one entrance to the residence? Does it have a mother-in-law apartment with its own kitchen, bath, and entry? All these things make it that much easier to turn it into a rooming house type of rental. If none of these already exist, can they be added fairly inexpensively where you could recoup the cost of investment rather quickly? It's something to consider.

If you can get $500 – $1,000 a month in added income by renting part of your existing property, would that make a significant difference to your family's budget? Yes, it would! If you're about to lose your house because you're starting to fall behind on your mortgage or you've just lost your job, couldn't this be a way to help make up some or all of the shortfall and help you to keep your home? Of course it could!!

Nobody says you have to do this forever; you can stop renting as soon as you want or you can wait until your financial situation improves enough to make it work for you and your family again.

Just be sure to give your tenants proper notice once you've decided not to rent to them anymore. Always treat your tenants fairly and professionally, as you would want to be treated.

CHAPTER 8
Combining Households, A Real-World Example

Maybe having a bunch of rental property isn't right for you; but you still like the idea of having more cash flow at the end of the month.

My friend Peggy has a large, four-bedroom home that she and her dogs have lived in by themselves for many years. She has a friend who she has known for a long time who also has a dog. They decided to move in together and share Peggy's large home; they are roommates.

Without realizing it, they are making better use of the property—maximizing the property's potential and its use, as I mentioned earlier—but they are also doing much more than that. They have each cut their living expenses significantly and have increased their quality of life. When one is home, the other is usually out of the house working, so they still get the benefits of having the 'house to themselves.' Her new roommate, in exchange for paying rent, helps to maintain the house and property and takes care of Peggy's dogs while she is working. Peggy is more at ease now, knowing that there is someone at the property taking care of her dogs who she knows will actually care for their needs and well-being. Instead of each of them going home to an almost empty house, by combining households, they literally never come home to find there is no one there to greet them. Having someone else to communicate and emphasize with is vital to a long and healthy lifestyle. They both have gained much more than just a significant increase in their personal cash flow each month.

As our society ages, specifically as the baby-boomers move further into retirement, I see the need for this type of companionship-style housing to increase dramatically. If it hasn't already started on a larger scale, it will in the next decade. Who wants to come home to an empty house? Maybe the kids are grown and gone? You're now an empty-nester? What do you do? What if your spouse has passed on? What if you're elderly, have a medical issue and there is no one nearby? No one who comes to check on you? There have been too many stories of this exact same thing happening in our society, and if people are willing to rent out their home or leave their home and live with someone else, this can be a way where everyone benefits in the long run.

CHAPTER 9
Combining Households, Another Real-World Example

Here's another example of how combining households can maximize a property's potential.

Things can change over the years when owning a property. I have a property that is quite large; it is a six-bedroom, three-bathroom home of about 4,000 square feet. For many years, I rented the entire property to individual tenants and that worked extremely well. Now that I have a family that has grown, we have expanded our household to use the entire upper level. We decided many years ago that since we had so much space in the upper level portion of the property, we didn't really need the use of the lower level, except to do our laundry. The lower level consists of two bedrooms, a bathroom, and a living room/dining room combination. At about 1,500 square feet, it is as large as many individual homes and was really just a lot of extra space; if it was used by just us, it wouldn't be used to its maximum potential.

This lower level is easily accessible since it has a walk-out entry on the front of the house. We have rented one of the rooms to a grandmother, who over the years has now become like a grandmother to our children. The other room has been rented to a longtime friend of mine who is in a transitional period in his life and needed to reduce his costs.

It works out well for everyone. Without any additional strain on our space or living conditions, we have still managed to keep some of the additional income I had when it was rented out to individuals and we have provided for two additional households to share our extra available space. They have both been able to reduce their living expenses while still being able to live in a home; they have their own space and yet we share many things together. We often interact either inside the property, watching a movie or sharing a dinner, or outside in the yard over a bonfire or around the backyard grill.

Someone is almost always home and yet, we each feel like we have our own private living areas.

Again, this may or may not be for you, but these examples may give you some ideas on what you can do with your current property or the property you buy in the future. If you buy it right, it can be adjusted to suit your needs as things change in your life.

By providing you with these real-world examples, I wanted you to know that I am doing exactly what I have been describing in this book and have been doing so successfully for many years! You can too!

CHAPTER 10
Why This Might Not Be For Me

No matter what type of business you have, there are going to be problems, overheads, and tradeoffs—you just can't change this fact. Every business is different and has its own challenges; but given the choice of being a business owner or having a job, I would much rather be a business owner in control of my own destiny!

I do not want to scare you away from this opportunity, but this business may not be a *good fit* for you. Many books on real estate pretty much say that anyone can be a successful investor. That's not always entirely true. It takes a certain type of person to invest in real estate and this type of real estate—rooming houses—is no exception. You may or may not be the type of person who can manage this kind of investment. Here are some of my reasons behind this thought:

Management

This type of real estate investing is more management intensive than others. Since renting is going to either be in your primary residence or a secondary property that you've bought specifically to invest in, you will probably be doing most of the management yourself, especially when you're just starting out. Since you are dealing with numerous and diverse people, depending on the renting/housing code of the city you live in, you have automatically increased the amount of time it takes to manage a property. Each person is an individual tenant and will need special attention from time to time. Problem solving, maintenance issues, rent collection, and other issues will consume many hours of your free time. Whereas, if you were to rent a property to only one person or one family you only have one other person or a couple of people to deal with. So, if you aren't interested in managing people and aren't a good *people person* this business may not be for you. Although, on the other hand, if you want to gain those skills of being a *people person* and managing property, this can be a good way to build those skills and earn your real estate PhD, on a small scale.

Managing your own properties can also take up more of your free time—time that you could be spending with your friends and family or doing the other things in life you love to do. If you manage your properties well, you can minimize time spent and still be able to devote to your attention to other activities; if not, then you might want to proceed with caution.

I had no idea if I had the necessary skills, until I started renting out my own property. If it didn't work out, I knew that I could just give my tenants proper notice and then the house space would be completely mine again. Starting with my own home eliminated the risk of buying another property, only to find that this business didn't suit me.

Community size

You will definitely do better in this business if you have a larger pool of people to draw from for potential tenants. Larger cities work best for this; however, you might be in a small city or town that has a large transient or temporary population who need temporary housing. If so, then this style of rental housing could work well for you.

Don't get me wrong, I love small towns—I'm from one—but the problem with smaller towns is they may be entirely dependent on only one or two major industries and those major industries may be very interdependent on each other. If one goes, the other may go— and your real estate investments may go too. So keep that in mind, if you're buying in a smaller town. Always look for viable locations in dynamic towns. For example, I would always be more inclined to invest in a college or university town than in a quiet farming community. Capital cities and military towns are good bets, but exercise caution with the latter.

Also, rents do not go up as often in small towns as they do in larger cities. You want your rents to go up as fast as they can so that your cash flow increases as fast as it can.

Do I want to rent out my primary residence?

As previously mentioned, you may not want to have renters in your private space, your home. If that is the case, then you may need to pursue purchasing a separate home to rent. If you're sharing the same home with one or more people, you will be having day-to-day interactions with them. You may want more privacy, more *quiet time*. This is very important and something to keep in mind. You'll sort out many of these questions very quickly and can change your rental policies as needed.

Whenever I have tenants sharing the same common spaces in my home, I keep all of my valuable items in my own private suite. I live in the master bedroom to have the larger space. Items get broken no matter how careful people are. If it's something near and dear to me, I want to safeguard it as much as possible.

Do I want to be an absentee landlord?

If you decide at some point to purchase a property that you do not live in and your portfolio and/or cash flow isn't large enough to pay someone else to manage it, then you will become an *absentee landlord*. Once you become an absentee landlord, things change. The tenants know you do not live there and that you aren't at the property on a daily basis and the number of things that can happen increase. The frequency of these things happening depends on the type of tenants you have at the property. If they aren't the best type of tenants, then of course you will have more problems. I noticed this happening when more people were buying houses a few years ago. Many of the remaining tenants who were looking for rooms to rent were those who couldn't qualify for other types of housing. Today, a number of factors impact the tenant pool. These include the housing situation the way it is, and the difficulty in qualifying for a mortgage and purchasing a home of their own or the cost and availability of apartments. The quality of the tenant pool has improved significantly. Everything ebbs and flows the longer you're in any business; and as time moves on, you'll notice a variety of patterns emerge.

For example, I have had a couple of tenants who were arguing; they were in the habit of calling me in the middle of the night to tell me that since they can't sleep, they thought I shouldn't be able to either. Is that something you're willing to put up with? No, neither could I. I resolved the issue the tenants had with each other; then I gave that tenant who called me a warning and told him if it ever happened again, I would be giving him his notice. I also went out and bought myself a phone that would allow me to turn off the ringer when I go to bed. Problem solved. If it's a real emergency, they can call 911. Otherwise, problems like this are better dealt with during regular business hours.

Summary

Give careful thought to this type of investing. At the end of the day, it comes down to what you want out of life and what you're willing to do to get there. If you're willing to make some small sacrifices and work a little harder in the short term for greater cash flow, then this could be your path to success. This book can help you do that!

CHAPTER 11
What To Do First

A suggestion

Even with today's fancy, do-everything technology, it's still a good idea to have a back-up file (data) of all the electronic information close at hand. I'm more old school, so I have found it a great help to have an actual planner, preferably with a zipper, that I carry with me wherever I go. A good one will cost about $50; the yearly refills are about $30. In it, I record all the vital information regarding each property—appliance repair data, brands and manufacturing numbers, bulb sizes, furnace filter sizes, and the property's tax ID number. It has been very helpful over the years to have all this information available at a quick glance. A good planner has spots for letters, bills to be paid, important documents, and so forth. It is a handy tool that will quickly become indispensible.

Research

First: *Read this book!*

Second: Take classes and seminars on how to run your own business, such as small business accounting basics and strategies. There are a lot of books and classes that can help you through these necessary basics. This book is a great piece of your real estate library, but do not stop there. Read, read, and read some more!

Third: Study the geographical area where you intend to invest. What are the schools like? How many are there? How close/far away from your property are they? Who are the big employers in your area? What options do tenants have for alternate transportation? For entertainment? What are the options for accessibility to healthcare, parks, and recreation? Why would tenants want to rent in that area versus another area? These are just some of the questions you should consider before investing in a particular area.

Once you've done the above and feel that you're ready to take the next step, then it's time to start building your team.

Building your team

This is vital to anyone's success. Your team will be made up of different people, but those people are key in your development as a real-estate investor. You cannot do everything yourself and you shouldn't try to, either. You must depend on those around you who have special skills, talents, and expertise. Bankers, mortgage brokers, insurance agents, property maintenance people, and other professionals are all important to your continued growth and success.

If you have family members who are supportive, start there. For me, my family was my moral compass, my support team, and the people who helped me as I got started. To them, it didn't matter what I did—they were there supporting me no matter what my ideas were.

I read many, many books on real estate before I felt I was ready to start investing, but what helped me most was having a mentor. My mentor was my landlord, Larry. Years ago, I was renting from him and he was willing to be my mentor. He was someone who I could measure myself against. He was very successful in this business and brought to life many of the things I had studied. He welcomed my questions and was always happy to help me find the answers. For many years, whenever something unexpected would pop up, I would ask Larry what he had done—what worked for him and what hadn't. That's the type of mentor you need to look for. Referring to this book can also help answer a lot of the questions you may have.

You'll start with a supporting family, a mentor, and a team of professionals on your side—people who will be a sounding board for your thoughts, your ideas, and your problems as your business grows.

It will be advantageous to continue adding more people to your team, to refine it perhaps. Lawyers, accountants, realtors, mortgage brokers/bankers, etc. are all critical members of a winning enterprise. When it comes to your team, there really are no limits to how many or who they are.

Finding the kind of people to have on your team is often the most difficult part, because you do not want just any accountant, lawyer, or realtor representing you. You want people on your team who believe in you and who understand what you're trying to accomplish. It's even better if you can find people who specialize in the type of real estate you're investing in or who have other clients in the same or similar businesses, because they will be better able to understand you and what you're trying to accomplish.

On occasion I have dealt with banks and mortgage brokers who had a hard time visualizing rooming houses and what they were until I went over it with them in detail.

For you it may start with someone else, but for me it was my mentor who referred me to the next great asset on my team. My realtor. At the time I was introduced to Christy, I had already had transactions with other realtors in the past while starting my business, but my business really took off when my mentor referred me to a realtor he had met. I knew during our very first meeting that I had found the next great asset for my team. Christy was someone who knew exactly what I was about, who believed in me, and who was also a real-estate investor.

She brought excellent real-estate services, superb attention to detail, access to her network of contacts and experts, and the essential quality necessary in team members—belief in my business plan and wanting to help me accomplish it. You must have people on your team who believe in what your vision is; if they do not, then you're not getting the best person for you or your team. This is not always evident—as your business matures, you will modify your team. Some will stay, others will go. Not everyone shares your dream. Few have the foresight; even fewer have the tenacity.

But for me, I knew early on that Christy was someone who would be a huge plus to have on my team. She has proven me right time and time again. For example, through her, I found one of my first, multi-talented maintenance men. She has been an endless resource of quality referrals for just about any type of service or repair I need on my properties. If you can find people like Christy to have on your team, it will mean much less footwork for you, and much more time and money saved. Your team members have already sorted out many different service providers and are ready to pass on that knowledge to you.

Through the references/referrals you have at this point, it should be easy to add others, like accountants, mortgage brokers, maintenance/repair people, etc.

It will take time to build both a professional team and a service team. Start small. Build as you go. Ask everyone for referrals. In time, you'll find the right people. Do not worry if you do not have all of these people right away; as long as you have one or two, the others will follow faster than you realize. So do not let this stop you from continuing with the next step.

CHAPTER 12
What To Do Second

Get preapproved

This means you need to know exactly your *borrowing power*. How good is your credit? You must know exactly how expensive a property you can purchase based on your credit, your income, other assets, and your debt-to-income ratio.

What is your debt level compared to your income?

I cannot stress this enough. Get preapproved before you take one foot out the door to look at properties. I have done this each and every time I start looking for a property and won't do it any other way. No matter how excited you are about investing, it won't do you any good to start looking at properties if you can't qualify to purchase them. Too many people start looking at a property to purchase either for themselves or as an investment without getting preapproved. They find a property they're in love with and find out after getting into the paperwork and financing that they do not qualify to purchase it. This is disappointing and you've lost a lot of time by skipping the "preapproval" step. You've not only wasted your time, you've wasted the valuable time of your realtor as well and other members of your team. If you want people to respect you, then you have to respect them as well, and part of that is knowing that their time is valuable.

Now, if you're smart and get preapproved ahead of time, you will know exactly how much property you can afford—and as soon as you've found a property in that price range, you'll be ready to make an offer. This has also worked to my advantage since being preapproved; my offers get accepted faster by sellers. They know I mean business and I'm ready to close on the property.

Believe me, getting preapproved ahead of time clarifies your position and provides reliable guidance for beginning the important step of searching for properties.

Fixed rate or ARM?

I also advise you to get preapproved with a fixed-rate mortgage versus an adjustable-rate mortgage. With a fixed-rate mortgage, you know exactly what your monthly mortgage payment is going to be today, tomorrow, and all through the length of your mortgage—it does not change unless you have hazard insurance and property taxes included in your payment. On the other hand, if you have an adjustable-rate mortgage (ARM), it usually starts off with a nice teaser rate; however, they usually go way up later on. This can be a significant impact on your cash flow. I want to know what my cash flow is today and what it is going to be throughout the length of my mortgage, that's why I have always gone with fixed-rate mortgages. Many people today have lost their properties because they were enticed by the initial monthly savings an ARM provides; but some of them failed to consider the long-term impact a rate increase from an ARM could do. If at all possible, avoid ARMs!

CHAPTER 13
What Next?

After you've started building your team and you're preapproved, what next? Searching and selecting the property that fits your needs.

Appreciation vs. cash flow

You will often meet people who will try to tell you to buy a piece of property for its appreciation potential. Do not buy into it. Never, ever buy real estate for this reason alone. Your main reason to purchase should be good, positive cash flow and the hope that it appreciates; if it does, then great, you're ahead of the game. But when it comes down to it, as long as its cash flowing well, then you do not need to ever worry about it appreciating. Appreciation will take care of itself.

Many people were buying property during the last boom under the assumption that real estate always appreciates. I attended a few seminars during this boom period and the speakers were all selling residential investment property which had negative cash flow and boosters were projecting that it would appreciate very fast and still be a good investment. This is "speculation." Well, look at our economy now. We've seen severe depreciation in real estate. Most of the people who purchased those negative-cash-flowing properties are struggling now or have even been foreclosed upon. Always, always, buy for the cash flow. If properties depreciate, you can still produce a positive cash flow even if you have to lower the rents. Something to keep in mind.

Type of property to invest in

I have looked at thousands of properties to purchase over the years and have come up with my own system for what type of property works best for me and my investment style. This may not be what works best for you in the location you choose. I have found that it helps to reduce the potential for problems later on if you find a system that works and stick with it. Start out using my pattern and plan to expand it and create your own "model" as you go along.

Below are the main criteria I look for in a property and why it is important.

Single family houses

I like single family houses because you can have three or four bedrooms to rent out and still have plenty of room for yourself and your family. This doesn't work as well with apartments, condos, duplexes, etc. These other types of real estate can limit the number of bedrooms you can rent or sublet since they have clauses in their leases restricting this. Many condo complexes and apartment buildings limit how many units can be non-homeowner occupied as well. Their associations may also restrict this.

Single family houses usually aren't limited by associations or clauses in leases, although there are neighborhoods with restrictions. Most areas are usually only limited by the renting/housing ordinances in the city or town in which they are located. Before you buy, check with your city or town and find out how many unrelated people can live at that address. For example, if you purchase a property you really like in the city you live in and then find out you can only rent to two unrelated people, you're going to have a hard time getting the house or your investment to cash flow by renting out the rooms. On the other hand, if you find out that you can rent to four, five, or six people, you will have a much easier time getting the property to cash flow and cash flow well. The more people you can legally rent to, the greater your cash flow will be!!!

City or suburbs?

I prefer to purchase my properties in the suburbs over the inner cities. The lower risk of maintenance issues combined with more stable tenancy help my cash flow remain dependable. I find these properties are often constructed more recently and have newer basic appliances. They also have larger rooms which rent more easily. Again, it depends on the property you're looking at and its potential; so do not rule out a location just because it's in the city or vice versa. Just remember, you want properties in close proximity to each other for ease of maintenance, travel time, etc. (More on this later on in this chapter.)

Style

Typically, I look for a three- or four-bedroom house, about 2,000 square feet, which has at least two to three bathrooms. This is your standard suburban home in the Midwest. Most people will look at a house like this and see only one renter or one family to rent to; I look at it a little differently and see four, five, or even six separate tenants, each paying me rent every month.

These houses typically are ranch-style (one level), split-entry or rambler-type houses. They are usually not located on a busy street but are within a block or two of a busy street for bus and transportation accessibility. Although depending on the lot size, location, value or some other factor, I have bought them on busier streets. You will only know this with experience whether or not this works for your tenants.

The houses usually have two to three bedrooms upstairs and one or two downstairs—or at least enough space in the basement or the rest of the property for an additional one or two bedrooms to be added.

Exterior

Usually the exterior of the property is wood, brick, vinyl, or steel siding. I stay away from stucco-type siding on properties; it can require more maintenance and I'm always looking for the least amount of maintenance as possible. If a stucco-covered house is very inexpensive to buy, its potential to create long-term, positive cash flow may offset the maintenance risks.

Very little renovation/repairs

I typically purchase properties that don't require a lot of work to get them rented out. I want to purchase something that is immediately ready to be rented or will only need minor repairs or cosmetic modifications. If you have to do extensive renovations on a property it can substantially affect your cash flow, especially early on while the repairs are taking place.

For example, the first property I purchased was a four-bedroom house that I bought and immediately moved into; I began renting rooms a month later. I didn't have to do anything to get it ready to rent—it was later on, when I wanted to increase my cash flow, that I made some modifications to the house.

If you have to make major repairs to the property, it can cause delays in getting it rented right away. This can still work, as long as you budget for it. It is not something I have chosen to do because I strive for immediate and maximum cash flow.

Bathrooms

There are always at least two bathrooms—one upstairs and one downstairs—in the properties I purchase. At a minimum, you'll want two bathrooms; anything less will turn off your potential tenants, especially if you're renting to four or more people. The more bathrooms the property has, the greater chance that a bedroom or two will have its own private bathroom. This is ideal for this kind of rental property and gives a significant boost to your bottom line. As previously mentioned in Chapter 3, if you have two rooms of the same size, but one of them has its own bathroom, that could be an increase of as much as $100 per month on that room. People who rent these rooms with private baths also tend to stay longer since they have their own mini-apartment at a much lower cost than renting a normal apartment. If you can find a house that has as many bathrooms as bedrooms, you have the potential to significantly increase your cash flow. These are hard to find at anything approaching a "reasonable price," but if you find one, grab it and add it to your portfolio.

Yard

The house in my example usually has a standard-sized city/suburban lot for a yard. It doesn't have to be much, just big enough for your tenants to enjoy during the warm months. The yard space also makes the place feel more like home and that is another goal to accomplish. The happier the tenant, the longer they will continue to rent from you.

Fencing

Since these types of rental property aren't being set up to rent to families with kids or pets, fencing is not a necessity. If the property has a fence and everything else meets your parameters, then consider it is a bonus when it comes time to sell; however, fences actually are another expense to owning a property since they are occasionally in need of repair and require more diligence when it comes to lawn care.

Garage

The kind of properties I look for have at least a two-car garage. Garages can be attached or freestanding. Garages are a great source of extra cash flow as well. Each garage space/stall, depending on the city or town you live in, can be anywhere from $25 per month up to $100 per month—and even higher amounts can be appropriate in larger cities. I love garages and try to get properties with as many as possible; tenants love them too. Garages keep their vehicles free of snow and debris; they provide shade from high temperatures in the summer, and they help to minimize vandalism. The additional storage space a garage provides is beneficial too. Tenants renting garage stalls also tend to stay longer at your property. Again, this is what you want.

Driveway

I usually pay extra attention to the size, shape, and condition of the driveway. It must be large enough to accommodate multiple vehicles—perhaps five, six, or more. If that space isn't there, is there room to expand? It's not good if the cars "stack up," meaning that I want tenants to be able to get in and out of the driveway at any time they wish with as little hassle as possible. When I was a tenant living in rooming houses, I had to knock on doors, trying to get people to move their vehicle when I needed to get in or out and it's not fun, especially when you're in a hurry. By having enough space so everyone can come and go whenever they want, convenience goes up and tension goes down.

Off-street parking

Many cities and towns, especially suburbs, have ordinances that do not allow *on-street* parking during the early morning hours, usually between 2:00 and 6:00 a.m. This allows the city to do sweeps for abandoned vehicles and also keeps the neighborhood looking clean and organized. Having a place for tenants to park all their cars off the street means you stay in compliance with city ordinances; this also helps keep your neighbors satisfied that your tenants aren't going to always be parking in front of their homes. I require my tenants to either park in the driveway or in front of the immediate property and nowhere else. I also prefer tenants' guests to park in front of the property as well.

Driveway material and size

If you have to widen the driveway on your property, which I've had to do in many of my locations, be sure to check with the city on the ordinance for driveways. Usually the driveway has to be asphalt, pavers, cement, or class five; it cannot be just the grass and dirt that's been there all along. You will also need to find out how wide the driveway can be and if it can run up against the property line of the neighbors lot (if applicable). You might need a waiver from your neighbor to allow this and some neighbors may not be too happy knowing that you're widening the driveway because you plan on having multiple tenants at the property. Usually, the apron (section where the driveway meets the street) at the bottom of your driveway cannot be widened, so your addition to the driveway will probably have to be tapered down to meet the apron size. This is important because it can limit the size of the driveway addition and may decrease the size of your driveway by at least one car. Although this doesn't sound like a lot, it can be significant. Every tenant wants to have their vehicle inside a garage or off the street, so if one tenant is forced to park on the street, it increases the chances of something happening to the vehicle; and again, you don't want to violate a city ordinance limiting on-street parking.

As an example, one time when I was renting, I had to park my car on the street since the driveway was not large enough to accommodate my car and another tenant's car. I had a really nice sports car; fortunately, I had just put it in storage for the winter. My winter beater was an old pickup, which I parked on the street exactly where I had parked the sports car a few days before. Later that night, outside my window, I heard a loud noise as a car went by. I didn't think too much about it since it just sounded like a crushed aluminum can flipping down the street. The next morning, as I went around my truck to get in, I noticed that my driver's-side mirror was missing. Looking around, I found it lying on the street about twenty feet away, with broken and shattered glass clinging to it. That smack I heard the night before must have been from someone getting too close and clipping it off my truck. Since it was just my old beater truck, I didn't worry about it too much; I got an old mirror to replace it at a local junkyard. But if it was my fancy sports car, it could have been much more expensive, since the mirror and the door was combined in one piece of molded plastic. The expense of replacing *that* could have run me many hundreds of dollars. So you can see the importance of having ample driveway and garage parking available.

Driveway expansion

When I've had to widen driveways, I've usually used asphalt for the sole reason that it's economically less expensive to install than concrete or pavers; and it stays in place more easily than class five, the cheapest alternative. Class five consists of crushed rocks; it will move over time as people maneuver their vehicles in and out of the driveway. When you have to snow blow your driveway or have it plowed in the winter, the class five will move as well. The last thing you want is for your snow blower to pick up a rock and launch it through one of your tenant's car windows, your house window, or your neighbor's window. So although asphalt may be more expensive, it is a better investment than class five.

I also prefer driveways that have as horizontal a grade to them as possible. Other features being the same when comparing one house to another, I will always choose the house with the more horizontal driveway than the one that is more inclined. While it doesn't seem like a big deal, horizontal driveways make it easier to park vehicles and they are easier to use. If you plan on having property in the colder climate areas of the world, the more flat the driveway is, the easier it is to use during winter. It's hard enough to keep from slipping and falling in the winter on a flat driveway, let alone one that is on a hill or even at a slight grade.

Accessibility

Many of the tenants I rent to are people who do not have their own transportation and therefore rely on public modes; so it is important that your properties are as close to public transportation as possible. All of my properties are either on a bus line or within a mile of it. I love tenants who do not have their own transportation—not only does it reduce the number of vehicles in the driveway, making it easier for the other tenants, but it more than likely means this tenant will stay longer. It can sometimes be hard to find adequate, reasonably-priced housing near public transportation. People know this and are happy when they find a place that is accommodating to them and their needs.

Location

As they say, *"location, location, location"* is the main rule in real estate. Investing in this type of real estate is no different in that respect. Other desirable amenities include proximity to businesses, schools, and entertainment.

Some authors will recommend purchasing real estate within a 50-mile radius of your home. That may be fine when you're having someone else manage it and you only drive by it once or twice a year; but if you're going to be doing the managing and you're going to be showing the rooms to prospective tenants yourself, I suggest that you keep them all closer together. Less than 10 miles from where you live is ideal; more than 10 miles and you're going to be driving to all your locations and putting a lot of mileage on your vehicle. The furthest investment property I own, from my residence, is just 6 miles away and it still takes about a half-hour of drive time (15 minutes there and 15 minutes back). So the closer the better!

By staying within the 10-mile limit, I can drive by my properties frequently. I see the goings-on at my properties and at other potential investment properties in the area. I know what other properties are selling for. When I see a bargain, I'm ready to go. I'm preapproved and can make an offer quickly.

That's another reason to be preapproved at all times, even if you're not quite ready to buy. When you see a positive-cash-flowing investment property, you'll be ready to move fast. If you're prepared to act, and act fast when the deals surface, you'll be well rewarded for your efforts.

Amenities and services

The closer you are to schools, restaurants, airports, shopping, etc. the better suited your properties will be for tenants as well. If they can walk to these locations, even better since some of your tenants won't have their own transportation. If at all possible, just don't buy your property under the flight path(s) of a major runway. This is part of the amenity that tenants don't want to have access to that often. Same thing applies to trains.

CHAPTER 14
Picking The Right Property

The right city to invest in

You know the saying, "Knowing what I know now, I wish I would have known then." Well, that applied to me and should apply to you as well. If I had checked with one of the cities before I started investing there, I would have found out that this particular city only allows a maximum of four unrelated people living at the property; other cities that border this city allow more. So because of this big unknown it cost me a minimum of an extra $450 per month—that's $5,400 a year! That's money that would have made my property cash flow that much more. The property still cash flows, but it could have cash flowed much better had I known that valuable piece of information.

So don't make this mistake. Be sure to check the city's ordinances on renting to non-related people before you even start looking at properties.

Do not purchase the first property that comes along

Now that you know the criteria of what you're looking for, it's time to find the right property.

I suggest that you start looking for the property that meets your criteria and that you keep on looking. Do not purchase the first house that you *think* meets your criteria; look at many more, so that you know *exactly* what fits. Then, if you find the first property turned out to be the one that fit your criteria more precisely than the others, go back and make an offer on it. It may or may not still be available, and you may feel that you've missed out on the opportunity of a lifetime, but don't worry, since you're now looking more closely at these properties that meet your criteria, you are getting more knowledgeable every day and can spot the next good deal more easily. There will always be another "opportunity of a lifetime" property just down the road.

CHAPTER 15
Making An Offer

Once you've found the property that meets your criteria, it's time to make an offer. Making an offer on a residential property depends on the area it's in, the location relative to everything else, its age, its condition, and the current real estate and rental market in that area. Over the years, I've made offers in all different environments with all different locations and conditions of properties. During today's economy, it is fairly easy to get a beautiful property in excellent condition well below the fair market value of the property; in years past, during the height of the real estate boom, I had to pay the asking price for a property and I've even been involved in bidding wars. While I do not recommend paying more than the asking price for a property, in some cases it is justifiable as long as your cash flow numbers still work at the new, higher price. In this particular case, I still own this property and it is one of my best income earners, even at the inflated price I paid for it years ago.

I'm going to repeat what I said in an earlier chapter. Do not ever buy an investment property that will not cash flow from day one!! During the heyday of real estate a few years ago, I attended a few seminars from time to time and sometimes would come across these salesmen saying how great the property was but it didn't cash flow right now!!! What? If it didn't cash flow right now, at this great time to invest in real estate, what would happen when the market turned for the worse? They said "not to worry about it because the value would keep going up." When I heard that, I knew right then and there I didn't want to invest with them either; and this was a room full of bankers, realtors, and seasoned investors who were working with this investment company! Well, I bet they're not doing so great now! I'll say it again: do *not* ever buy an investment property if it's not going to cash flow from day one!!!!

Look at the numbers and see where you stand. Consider how much cash flow a property will produce. Again, this is where being preapproved comes in handy. I already know from my preapproval what my monthly expenses are going to be based on a mortgage for the preapproval amount. Knowing this, I'm already looking at properties that will cash flow. So, the lowest price I can get the property for, the more it will cash flow. For some, the offer isn't low enough unless it insults the owner; for others, the offer should be high enough so it almost insults the owner. I think the best result has been for me to make an offer that is realistic. For example, if I'm preapproved for a property up to $200,000, I'm usually not going to *low ball* the seller at $100,000 unless there is something seriously wrong with the property. If it's not clearly evident there is something wrong with the property, a thorough inspection will identify problems and allow a basis for negotiating a more realistic price. Every deal is different. If you know how much the seller really needs, his *bottom line*, you may find an even lower price. I always start lower knowing that I have room to increase my offer. Other factors may affect this property as well (i.e. the local economy, multiple offers, etc.); therefore, I'd make a starting offer of $150,000. Remember, I already know that my property will cash flow and cash flow well at $200,000. If I can purchase it for less, my positive cash flow will be even higher each month.

Many people today are upside-down or "under water" with their mortgages. As a result, they are forced to list their homes at a high price. In such cases, lower offers will be impossible for them to accept; but if the property is vacant, it may be bank owned and you should start your offer much lower than even my example. It's okay, insult the bank with a low offer; they're not going to take it personally. They have a huge amount of properties on the books and need to sell them. Have your realtor check to see if there are other offers on the property, and then adjust your offer accordingly.

Earnest money

Earnest money is usually an amount of money you put down on a property as you make the offer. This lets the seller know that your offer is serious. The standard is usually $1,000 per $100,000. So for a $250,000 property, you would put a minimum of $2,500 down. The more you put down, the more serious your offer looks to the seller.

As long as you don't back out of the offer for frivolous reasons, your earnest money goes towards your down payment on the loan, if you're financing. If you're not financing and just paying all in cash, then it just decreases the amount you need to bring to closing. You can get your entire earnest money refunded if you find something erroneous in the Seller's Disclosure or in the property inspection.

CHAPTER 16
Property Inspection

Inspection

Once you've gone through the offer process and you and the owner have agreed on a purchase price, it is now time to get the property inspected. *Always, have the property inspected by a licensed property inspector before purchasing the house.* If possible, you should go with the inspector. I have found it informative to attend the inspection. It can be very productive to ask the inspector about the things that concern him. It only takes a few hours of your time, but it is well worth it on such a large purchase. The seller shouldn't be there during the inspection. If he is, I suggest that you ask him to leave for a few hours. You are paying for the inspection and must have the full attention of the inspector. This is critical!!

I made the mistake of not having my very first property inspected. At the time, it all looked fine to me and I was buying it from a police officer. What could be wrong? It could have turned out terribly wrong for me. Fortunately, I was lucky and even all these years later it is still one of the best purchases I have made. But again, do not do what I did! Make it a point to spend the extra $300 – $500 to get each property inspected! It will be well worth the time and expense!

If during the inspection you find problems with the property, you now have the opportunity to go back and reduce your offer to cover the costs of the repairs or walk away from the deal completely. This is where the Seller's Disclosure is important. Every property you are considering purchasing should have a Seller's Disclosure that has been filled out by the seller, listing everything that is working and not working, included and not included with the property. If it has not been provided to you, then make sure you get one and compare it to the inspection report. Do they match? If not, and you've found more issues with the property than you want to deal with, you now have the right to walk away from the offer you've presented without any legal action against you or loss of your earnest money.

Each case is different for each property and it will depend on what you want to do with the property. If the repairs are minor and they won't affect you being able to cash flow the property immediately or soon after, then I would suggest renegotiation; but if the repairs are extensive, the costs will be significant. They will necessitate a renegotiation on the sale price, or they will break the deal.

On your first few properties my suggestion would be to just walk away and cancel the purchase agreement. Once you've become more experienced, you may want to tackle more challenging properties. Go ahead, but be cautious.

CHAPTER 17
Closing

Now that you've made an offer on a property, it's been accepted, and the inspection is done, the closing is next. Usually closings take place about 30 days after the offer has been finalized; but of course, this time period depends on the seller's needs, your needs, the terms of your agreement, and the time your team needs to meet legal obligations.

During the 30 days, it is a good time to gather the supplies you'll need to be ready once you're handed the keys. Prepare in advance what you will need to fix, repair, and/or improve the property. The items you will need to repair would be listed on your property inspection report.

For the closing itself, it is a good idea to have as many of your team members present as is possible, especially the first few times you close on a property. Mistakes get made, and if your team can help you review the documents as you're signing them, it will save you time, money, and headaches in the long run.

There is going to be a large amount of paperwork you're going to have to sign. Make sure you receive a copy of each and every page you've signed. Do not be in a hurry to sign. Take your time and read each page of every document carefully. If you don't understand something, now is the time to ask.

The mortgage company will require that you prepay a year's worth of property insurance at the closing. Have documents on hand showing that you've already prepaid this. Do not try to get this done at the closing. It will slow the process down or bring it to a halt. At this stage in the game, you want the closing to be finalized that day. Expect to pay about $700 for a $200,000 house.

Once the closing is finished and you have the keys, celebrate!!! You've just finalized the deal on one of the biggest achievements in life—owning cash-flowing investment property! I celebrate each and every one I've purchased!

CHAPTER 18
Suggestions For Preparing The House For Tenants

As briefly mentioned in Chapter 17, during the 30 days of the closing, it is wise to prepare many things in advance that you will need to have done at the property—that way, once the closing day has arrived, you're ready to go and can start making changes to the property immediately. Again, the idea is to be up and running as fast as possible to be able to cash flow as soon as you can.

Having new locks for the entrances and interior bedroom doors ready will save you time. Prepare your newspaper ad so that it runs shortly after you take possession. I usually like to run mine about a week or two after I take possession.

Line up any repairs and service upgrades as well. For example, many times the properties I've purchased don't have cable outlets in each bedroom. I want to upgrade the property so that all the bedrooms have this convenience immediately.

You'll need dishes, pots and pans, brooms, shovels, rakes, toilet bowl brushes, light bulbs, etc. It all depends on what you're willing to provide. I have provided some furniture. Tenants bring furniture. Tenants leave furniture behind. You'll have too much before long. It's all free. I have free, 12-year-old sofas still in great shape and still being used every day.

Some people like to start repairs before the closing date. I highly recommend against it, since the whole deal could be postponed or cancelled altogether; then you could be out your investment or at the very least have to wait to be reimbursed. If the seller isn't happy with what you did to their property, you could end up going to court over it. So, it's best to wait until the closing is finalized and you've got the keys before making any kind of repairs.

CHAPTER 19
How To Advertise And Attract Tenants

Advertise

People in this business advertise many different ways. Some landlords place ads in the local city papers that are more specific to their city/town; others will only advertise on the Internet; and still others sign up for roommate services. These are all great, but to get the largest pool of potential tenants, I prefer to advertise in the largest paper in the city/state. It usually has the largest daily readership in print and online and therefore the largest pool of potential tenants. I suggest you try a few different options and see what works best for your area.

From time to time I have also placed ads on the internet on sites like Craigslist (CL). I've had some luck this way, but again I want exposure to the largest amount of people possible, so that means I also want to target people who do not have access to the Internet; but with Internet traffic growing exponentially, I do continue to run ads on CL and other similar sites. You may even want to have a page on the social networking sites so that your business is exposed to this fast-growing group of potential tenants.

I've run my ads at different intervals: daily, two weeks at a time, and only on Sundays, for example. You'll have to test your market and see what works best for you. I've found that a combination of the weekly ads and multiple forms of media works best for my business.

Here is an example of what my typical ad looks like:

City/Suburb Shr Lrg House
$450/month incl. utilities, cable,
Internet, and cleaning service
Avail now. 612-123-4567

Feel free to use this example and modify it for your own use.

It is best to keep your ad short and to the point. If you have to use abbreviations to get everything to fit, then do so; but be sure those abbreviations are fairly easy to figure out, otherwise whenever someone contacts you the first question they will ask is, "what is 'no d/c alwd?'"

Did you figure out that abbreviation? No? It means: No dogs/cats allowed. If they've got a pet, then this just wastes your time and theirs, so abbreviate, but be clear.

Since there are a few people who place ads in the paper along with mine, I want mine to stand out from others, so I try to offer more services than my competition. This is no different than any other business. The successful businesses offer more for the same or better price. For example, I offer the extra cleaning services to help give the property a more consistent professional look. Some tenants clean, others don't. A service like this provides consistency and tenants will appreciate that added convenience.

For your business, it may be something else that the tenants want. Whatever option it is, you want to offer something different that will stand out in your ads, attract tenants, and help to keep tenants long term.

CHAPTER 20
Funding

Other than a couple suggestions below, I am not going to go into a lot of detail regarding funding, as there are numerous other real estate books that go into this and cover it just fine. I will say that if you're serious about buying real estate, keep going back, reapplying, keep asking until you gain success. Many, many times I have been turned down for funding, only to harden my resolve and not give up until I get what I want.

My first investment money came from cashing out my profit sharing and using the proceeds to fund my first property. That initial purchase has yielded about a 14,000% return over the years. While it worked for me, I do not recommend cashing out your 401K, your profit sharing, or your savings; but if you are going to cash it out, it is better to use the money to purchase a cash-flowing property or an appreciating asset than it is to use the funds to purchase depreciating assets, like cars, TVs, boats, etc. for general use. Sure, you'll get a lot of enjoyment out of them, but these toys do not put money in your pocket at the end of the day or food on the table, unless you use them for your profession. They just take money from you. I'd much rather use my funds to purchase cash-flowing property and then use that cash flow to purchase the toys and other consumer items we all want.

You could also ask your friends and family to invest in your business, but as I have found, most friends and family don't have extra money lying around to give to you. Although, this doesn't always work, you should exhaust all of your options. There's always "luck." A friend or relative may be looking for just such an investment opportunity and you won't know until you've asked. The only other downside to this option is that friends and relatives may want to become partners in your business. If you choose to go into business with friends and/or relatives, remember, not everything works out as planned, so make sure that both you and any financial backers are protected. Seek the advice and assistance of your team members when structuring any financial deal. You don't want bad blood to come between you and your business.

An idea I liked and thought about implementing was one I found in another real estate book. That author suggested taking $500 (or as much as you can feasibly come up with), go to a bank, and open a savings account. Deposit that $500 into the newly-opened account. Then come back a few days later and open a line of credit for $500 using the savings account as collateral. Take the cash from the line of credit to another bank and repeat the process until you've done this at five different banks. After a few months of having these accounts open and paying the minimal monthly payments on them, you go back and close the loans, paying a little bit of interest in each one. After you have done this, restart and repeat the process but increase the amount; except now you want to use your signature as the collateral, not the money in the savings account. The idea is to increase the amount of money you have for a down payment from $500 to $2,500 in less than a year with just using your signature.

Many years ago, I had started this same process and had opened my five accounts at five different banks. It was working perfectly for me, just as the book suggested. I did not continue with it since I found other avenues of getting my down payment money. But the idea was sound and was starting to work for me. Maybe it could work for you. Check it out for yourself. Don't rule out anything until you know the answer and whether it is something you want to pursue or not. In the end, you are smarter for knowing about it.

There are a lot of ways to get funding and these days it takes a lot more money for a down payment than when I started. Today you need 20% in most situations. That takes a while to save. In the end, it may be that you just have to save it a dollar at a time. It may take a while, but you will be proud of yourself for having undertaken the journey.

CHAPTER 21
Tenants

References

Tenants can make or break your business. I don't do a lot of screening of my tenants, just for the simple fact that screening is not a foolproof way to get good tenants.

As my friend Larry once said, "If you called me for a reference for X tenant and I really wanted them to move out, do you think I'm going to tell you that they were a bad tenant? Of course not. I'm going to tell you that they were terrific and I hate to see them go."

He was not advocating this of course, just highlighting the flaw in the system. The main reason I do not worry about references is that my leases are month by month. If I get a tenant who misrepresented themselves, I only have to give them a one-month's notice to move out. The same principle applies if the tenant moves in and they decide that this particular property and atmosphere is not right for them.

Month-by-month leases

The simplicity of this type of rental property is if you have a tenant or two who are becoming a problem, you can remove them faster from the property with a shorter month-by-month lease than you usually can when renting out the entire property on a yearly lease. Another great benefit is that the other tenants will usually let you know right away if someone at the property is being destructive or isn't getting along with everyone else.

I have always preferred the month-by-month lease over a six-month lease or one-year lease. As mentioned above, this is beneficial to both the landlord and the tenant. This does not mean that all of your tenants are going to move out every month. Happily, many of my tenants stay for years. Let's face it, people don't like to move. Moving is not fun. This is great for your business. Some tenants have rented with me continually for over ten years, in a month-by-month lease; in fact, many renters appreciate this type of lease simply because it allows them to opt out fairly quickly in case of a job relocation or a family crisis, etc. I have had many tenants who move in on the basis that they are only looking for three to six months and are intending to move on after that; many times, they end up staying on much longer. This also fills a void in the rental arena as most leases are one-year leases. This provides a great service to the tenants and the community.

You don't need a long, fancy lease from an office supply store to set this up; nor do you need one that looks like the ones you typically see in apartment rental offices. Those can be many pages long and you have to have the tenant put their initials on every page, sometimes multiple times. I prefer simple, quick, one-page leases that are perfectly legal and cover all your necessary terms quickly and easily. Your tenants will appreciate this as well.

For a sample of the type of lease I have used, I have included a copy of one with this book. See Appendix A. Whatever lease you use, for your protection as well as your tenants', you may want to have an attorney in your area review it and how it pertains to your business.

Eviction notice

This is one of the most important tools you as a landlord will ever employ. I give my tenants a grace period when it comes to paying rent each month, but once that grace period lapses, I am quick to give my tenants a Notice of Eviction. It simply states that they are to remove themselves from the property by the end of the month. Failure to do so will incur additional charges and possibly an Unlawful Detainer (which involves going to court). The "Notice of Eviction" also informs delinquent tenants that their credit history will be severely damaged. In most cases, a simple Eviction Notice will suffice to get the tenant to make other arrangements to pay, or move out.

Included is a sample I have used from time to time. Feel free to modify it as appropriate to your individual situation or to conform to county or state laws. See Appendix C.

Don't make the mistake of listening to all the sad stories of promises to pay. Before you know it, many months may pass with no rent to show for your generosity. In the end, you will still have to give them the eviction notice; but then, you will have not only lost that month's rent, you will have also lost many more months' rent—months that you could have been renting to *paying* tenants. So, buckle down. Be strong and assertive, professional, but still courteous.

If you make a mistake like this, the benefit is that it was only with one tenant. The rest of your tenants are still paying their rent and you are able to pay your other expenses, unlike if this were to happen when you rent out the entire house to one individual or one family. (Something else to keep in mind.)

Unlawful detainer

You can't physically remove an evicted tenant from your property. You must enlist the courts' help through a process called "Unlawful Detainer." It will require going to court and can be costly. In all the years I've been a landlord and with the hundreds of tenants I've had, only two delinquent tenants required this court action. Learn about these laws in your area. Prepare yourself for the times this might happen.

Filing an Unlawful Detainer varies with every state. Sometimes you can get the tenant removed rather quickly; in other cases, the process takes longer because the court system is more pro-tenant. Even so, having a month-by-month lease is invaluable in this case and will save you much time and money in the long run.

"Professional tenants"

I use this term loosely since it rarely happens, but the longer you're in this business, the greater the chance you'll encounter people who know how to work the system and who will try to take advantage of you. They are what I call *professional tenants*. They've been around, they know what to say and do when they move in, and then shortly thereafter stop paying rent and will try to cause all kinds of problems for you and your business. Getting references from previous landlords may prevent some of this from happening, but that is not a foolproof system either. (See the beginning of this chapter for my experiences and thoughts on getting references again.)

It is in your best interest to get them out of your property as soon as you can.

I wish I could say that it was easy to spot these professional renters, but it has proven to be difficult. Again, this is where having a month-by-month lease comes in very handy.

Be prepared in advance for what these professional renters will do. They do not care about you, your other tenants, or your business. All they care about is living at your property free of charge for as long as possible and then they move on to the next property and repeat the process again. It becomes a way of life for them. They will leave a mess behind for you to clean up or for you to have professionally cleaned up. On the next page are a couple pictures (Figs. 5 and 6) of what I was left with one time.

Figure 5 - Inside vacated tenant's bedroom

Figure 6 - Junk left behind

Just remember, this isn't the norm. You won't be having to clean up a mess this bad very often. It is part of the business. I only show these pictures to make you aware of what can potentially happen, whether you have references or not!

Smoking

I don't allow smoking inside the property for the obvious reasons that it's a fire hazard and also a health hazard to some people; but I do not exclude smokers, either. If you did that, you would significantly reduce a large portion of your potential pool of tenants. I let tenants smoke outside, as long as they do not leave a mess with their cigarette butts, etc. From time to time, I've had to talk to some tenants about smoking inside or the cleanup of their cigarette butts outside. After a couple times of this, if they don't or aren't willing to clean up after themselves, I ask them to move out. I don't think it's too much to ask to be thoughtful and courteous of the other tenants living there who are not smokers. Most people understand this and have been down that road before at previous places they have lived, but I put it in the lease and enforce it as much as is needed. It is a very important issue when many people are living together.

Shared spaces/common areas

In every house, there is shared space that all tenants can use as part of their lease. These areas are typically referred to as "common areas." These shared spaces, or common areas, tend to be the kitchen, living room(s), dining room, bathrooms, family rooms, etc. Basically, it is all rooms that are not the tenant's own private bedroom.

These spaces are great for people who have extra furniture or belongings they want to bring with them, whether it's a whole house of furniture, gym equipment, etc. down to just a chair or two. Most of the time people need more room for their possessions.

I tell all of my tenants that the shared space is for everyone to use; it's not exclusive to one person or a couple of people just because they have things in that room. I also tell them that if something is valuable, keep it out of common areas; keep it in their room.

Anything in the common areas is essentially available for everyone else to use. Other tenants should ask the owner of the item if it's okay to use it. Normally, food items are not shared.

These are the hardest areas to keep clean since everyone has access to them and almost no one will take the responsibility to clean them up. If you have a tenant or two who are very clean, they may even offer to keep it clean for you at no charge or maybe a small discount off their rent every month. This works well, depending on the tenant and of course if you are giving them a discount off of the rent, you'll have to keep an eye on it since some people will state they've cleaned the common areas but in fact haven't done much to justify the savings you're passing on to them. This is part of the reason why I have chosen to provide a separate, private cleaning service company as an extra service to the tenants. It keeps the place neat and I know that it's getting cleaned on a regular schedule.

Food and other consumables

Since food and other consumables are mostly kept in the common areas, it can sometimes be a 'grey area' for some people. Some tenants will simply use another tenant's food and not replace it, while others will go out of their way to prepare a meal for the other tenants at the property. Having multiple tenants at the same property can help to identify the problem tenant. If, after a tenant has talked with the problem tenant and it's still an issue, I will usually step in and make sure that things get resolved. If the tenant continues to use other people's food and isn't willing to replace or repay the other tenant, then I tell them this isn't the place for you and it's time to move on. I give them their Eviction Notice at the next available opportunity. This is actually a very small problem and doesn't happen as often as a person would think.

Some tenants prefer to have a small fridge and/or microwave in their room, which nullifies this problem as well. It will add to your electric bill a little bit, but if it keeps things calm, it's worth it.

Most of the time I'm renting to mature, responsible people who know how to conduct themselves around others and they do not cause problems. For those that do cause problems, you only have to give them one month's notice to move out and they are gone. Problem solved!

CHAPTER 22
Management Do's And Don'ts

Maintaining your professionalism

One thing many landlords forget is that they are in the customer service business. Your tenants are your customers, no matter if they are screaming at you at 3:00 in the morning or are complaining about something else going wrong at 3:00 in the afternoon. Always, always maintain your professionalism and always be polite. If your tenant(s) are screaming at you, screaming back at them will not resolve the issue; in fact, they will see how unprofessional you are and will probably move out after giving their notice. You do not want this to happen. It defeats the purpose of your business and that is to make money and to keep your tenants as happy as possible so they will in turn continue to rent from you.

In a rental situation such as this, you are not only showing the unhappy tenant how unprofessional you are, but you are also showing all the other tenants in the house who are nearby listening to your conversation with the disgruntled tenant how unprofessional you are. Remember, always assume your tenants are always watching and in this case listening. They will also see how you handle the confrontation and your reactions to it. In one moment, you could lose more than one tenant. This is not how to handle the situation.

Here's the proper way to handle this. Whenever a tenant has confronted me—and believe me, it has happened—I always maintain my composure; I respond politely, but with resolve and a firmness in my tone and actions, if I have to; then, I say something like this: "I will be happy to help you with your problem, but you must talk with me at a more normal level. I am being polite and professional with you. I expect the same in return. If, however, you do not want to talk to me in a more polite manner with a reasonable tone, then I will end this conversation right now." It may take a few tries, but time and again, being polite and professional wins at the end of the day. As the saying goes, *"Kill them with kindness and professionalism."* It is my *Modus Operandi* and it should be yours as well!

This book is packed with such good information, but doing this one thing will do a lot for your relationship with your tenants and will earn you their respect. You will find that as the years pass, many former tenants will want to rent from you again, mainly because of how professional and courteous you were to them!

To this day, most of my best referrals come from my previous tenants.

CHAPTER 23
Maintenance

For me, this comes down to simple economics. If it's something simple that I can replace or repair, then I will do it myself, saving the cost of having my maintenance man/handyman do the repair. For example, I always have a supply of light bulbs with me whenever I visit my properties. Whenever I see a bulb out, I simply reach in my truck and find a replacement. This saves me from having the tenant purchase a more expensive bulb, costing me a higher electric bill and/or having my maintenance man make a visit just to replace a bulb.

As another example, at the beginning of the month when it's time to collect the rent, I always bring along extra furnace filters and softener salt, thereby not only saving the expense of having my maintenance man do the job each month, but I know it's getting done on a regular basis and I am being proactive in prolonging the life of the furnace and the water softener.

When you start out with just your primary residence, or have just one or two other properties, you should always try to do as much of the minimal maintenance as you can, saving you the cost of having a repairman or maintenance man do the job. Depending on your ability, skill level, or inclination to get your hands dirty, it may be more productive to hire a professional.

As you move up and purchase more properties, time becomes more of an issue. I was working full time when I bought my fourth house and found that I had less and less time to get all of my maintenance repairs completed in a timely fashion. At that time, it started to make sense to have someone else help me with the repairs; so, I hired a maintenance man who was referred to me from one of the people on my team. I was able to focus more on managing the properties and the little repairs that I could tackle. Of course, this increases your expenses since the maintenance person charges more for his or her time than you do for your time, but they are also more experienced. In the end you'll save time and money. As time goes on, the maintenance person will become more familiar with what jobs you handle and what jobs he'll take care of. The maintenance person may take on more and more projects, perhaps some minor management issues as well.

I have had several maintenance men over the years and they have all proven themselves to be invaluable. Since they are an integral part of your team, make sure you pay them promptly. The next time you have an emergency, you'll get much better service.

Most times, I have found my maintenance men by referral and word of mouth. Sending out an email to all your contacts works as well. Sites such as CL also have many capable people listed. If you do find someone from a site such as this, who you don't know personally, get references and then check out some of their handiwork, if time permits. Try having them do a smaller job first so you can see the quality of their work.

You will want to sit down with your maintenance man and get to know him since he is an integral part of your business. You want someone who is going to compliment your business, not be a detriment to it. For example, since I try to be as courteous and professional as possible with my tenants, I definitely want a maintenance man working in my house(s) who is the same type of person. He is going to be around the tenants at all hours of the day and night; and how he behaves and conducts his job is a direct reflection on how well you manage your properties and your business. The beauty of it is that most people, certainly service industry people, know this and will conduct themselves accordingly since they want your ongoing and lucrative business. They want any and all future business from you.

CHAPTER 24
Appliance Repair

This is a must for rooming houses. Unless your profession is appliance repair, you will save a lot of money by having a service such as this for each property you own. For about $25 a month per property, it will cover the cost and repair to all your main appliances at the property. There are many types of these services out there and their prices do vary, so be cost conscious and compare pricing. These plans usually cover your furnace, air conditioning unit, water heater, washer, dryer, stove, range and fridge(s). Every plan is slightly different in what is automatically covered and what are considered add-ons that cost an additional $5 per month. These plans are well worth the cost. When you figure that the average repair can take anywhere from an hour to two hours, and the average part is around $25 – $50 dollars minimum, your repair bill can very quickly skyrocket into a few hundred dollars; but by having signed up for the appliance repair plan, your total cost is only the $25 per month!!! What a deal!!!

Learn from my mistake. One time I hadn't had a major repair in over six months and I thought I didn't need my appliance repair plans and removed them from all of my properties. I was thinking how smart I was on cutting my costs; then the very next week I had a major appliance break down at one of the properties. Total cost to fix the problem was $250!!! At $25 per month, I could have used that money for 10 months of appliance repair coverage on that property that would have covered ALL of my appliances!! What would have been my cost outlay if more than one appliance had gone haywire at around the same time? This does happen and will happen to you over time. So do the smart thing and get an appliance repair plan for all your properties. It's well worth the monthly cost.

In my research in comparing prices over the years, I have found many places that offer repair service plans. All are rather reasonable, but some are better than others. I would look for this service with companies around your home since they vary by location; but these days, your local electric and gas companies provide this service along with companies such as Sears and others in your area who specialize in appliance repair. Plans often come in mail advertising too. It's good to review and compare prices and values every few years.

CHAPTER 25
Unannounced Visits

Depending on how well the property is running, I will either make weekly visits to the property or only once a month. This can vary as renters move in and out of a property. Over the years, I have had some properties that I hardly ever visit except for once or twice a month; then when tenants turn over, I've had to rearrange my unannounced visits to make sure everything is going smoothly. This actually keeps the tenants on their toes since they are not sure when the landlord may show up. In the end, you'll spot problems before they get out of hand.

To be very clear, in rooming houses, landlords are only allowed to enter common area rooms in the property such as the living room, dining room, kitchen, unoccupied bathrooms, and storage rooms/garages, etc.

As with other types of real estate investing, private quarters— bedrooms, in this case—are not allowed to be entered by landlords without prior notice from tenants or 24 hours' notice by the landlord that you need to inspect. This can vary from state to state, so be sure to check with your state rental laws and the city/town in which you are investing. Emergency issues, damage, utility problems, etc., don't need a notice beforehand as long as these are stipulated in the lease. Once you know the laws, follow them exactly. The last thing you want to do is to invade someone's privacy and break the law when a simple phone call to the tenant or a note under the door giving them 24 hours' notice of entry would have sufficed. Again, be professional.

CHAPTER 26
Lawn Care / Snow Removal

When your business is smaller, it's easier and more economical to do these tasks yourself; as your business grows, they can take up much more of your time. It may be more economical to hire them out. I've done it both ways over the years. Some landlords have the tenants cut the grass and shovel the driveway, or do other chores in exchange for reduced rent. Be cautious if you experiment with a plan like this.

In order to ensure that the yard is maintained properly and the driveway is cleared quickly enough after snowstorms, I've hired professional services to handle these maintenance issues. You can cut your expenses dramatically by doing some of this work yourself. Lawn service companies will charge about $35 per lawn, which should include trimming and blowing grass clippings off the walks and driveway. In the winter you can expect to pay about $25 per driveway. These costs are on the low side of what I've found and used. Be careful about hiring maintenance services. A stormy season could be very costly, severely reducing your positive cash flow.

If you're investing in an area that is prone to more frequent and severe snow storms, like Buffalo, NY, it may be more cost effective to pay for snow removal monthly versus per occurrence.

If you invest in rooming houses in a cold weather zone, inevitably you will have to deal with snow. It's vitally important that you remove snow from the driveway and the walks as soon as possible and keep them free of snow and ice. The last thing you want is for one of your tenants to slip and fall on your property. If your maintenance philosophy is completely proactive, no one could suggest that you are negligent. Remember, you are in the customer service business and your tenants will see that you make every effort to see that things are done in a timely manner; they will see that you care about their comfort and safety and therefore care about them. This encourages continuous, long-term renters. If you don't maintain the driveways and walks promptly, your renters will move out. Again, remember you're in the customer service business. This is one more reason your renters will continue to add to your income flow each month.

CHAPTER 27
Pets

Cats

I usually do not allow cats, as some people are allergic to them and the cats need to be looked after. With so many people in a house, it can tend to get very crowded if everyone has a pet.

Cats and dogs are great pals, but unless your rental units are built to be "pet-proof" (i.e.: vinyl tile floors, no carpeting, no exposed wood, no furniture or sofas, etc.), you will have damages to deal with. I don't recommend having pets, but with some preliminary planning and preparation and a pet deposit, it can be successful.

Here's a story of why I do not allow cats at my properties anymore:

I made the exception one time to a fellow who was very passionate about his cat. He didn't want to get rid of the cat since he and the cat had been together for a very long time. He was even willing to pay my pet deposit of $200 and even pay extra each month so that he could keep the cat. After checking with all my other tenants to see if they were okay with it, I went ahead with the rental. At first, I thought my fears were unfounded because for the first year, all went well. In the second year, near the end of his occupancy, things changed. How come they always change near the end? lol.

In his haste to leave, he left everything behind. I spent the next few days cleaning up the mess. As I was moving the furniture around in the house, underneath the couch I found this man's scared and hungry cat! So much for it being so important to him that he couldn't live without it! Well, I couldn't very well leave the cat there, and I had no place for it. Not to mention the fact that I'm highly allergic to cats and dogs. I had to take the cat to the humane society. The cat knew something bad was happening. He fought me at every turn. Lesson learned, the hard way!

Dogs

My reasons for not allowing dogs are the same for cats: allergic tenants and the problems pets can bring with them. I love animals, but they are mostly high maintenance and aren't conducive to this type of rental lifestyle.

I haven't had as many problems with dogs as I've had with cats. Having a strict no pets policy in my lease has helped keep this to a minimum, but tenants will still try to sneak them in, even on a temporary basis. They've tried to hide them from me by keeping them in their rooms or they've kept them over the weekend while "helping out a friend." You name it, people will try it. You just have to keep on top of them or before you know it, your property will have plenty of animal-related problems. Again, that is where being able to drop by unannounced is invaluable!

Other pets

Over the years, I have had many tenants who've had other pets such as fish, lizards, birds, and small mammals/rodents. I don't mind these as long as they are quiet, their cages are kept clean, and they aren't left to roam outside the tenant's room. Again, keep the rules simple and clear and your tenants will respect the policy. Also, be consistent with your tenants.

CHAPTER 28
Insects And Other Pests

In just about any type of property, there are, from time to time, issues with insects. In each part of the world there are different types of insects and different ways of handling them. Since my properties are in the northern part of the United States, I'll keep my advice limited to them.

Ants are a problem just about every year. I've used many products to combat ants, but they still keep coming back. This is mostly due to poor cleaning habits of some tenants. No matter how many times tenants have been reminded of this fact, they continue to leave dirty dishes and food on the counters and in the sinks. Ants love a dirty house. I've had the best luck with the liquid ant bait that is placed on a small piece of cardboard. The ants gather up the sweet stuff and take it back to their nest, which in turn kills the whole colony within a few days. Problem solved.

Other insects

I have tried the sprays and the plug-in electric devices that are supposed to scare them away and nothing works as well as a bug bomb. The bug bombs usually come in a two or three pack. Normally, a once-a-year application is sufficient. Some houses never need that kind of care. After giving the tenants adequate notice to be away from the premises for a few hours, and reminding them that any food or sensitive electronics should be covered, I then turn off the gas appliances (yep, even the pilot lights) and let the bombs loose. I open all the interior doors in the house, usually place two in the basement and one upstairs and activate them and then quickly leave the premises myself. I usually stay onsite to watch the property and usually work on something else that needs to be repaired or resolved, thereby maximizing my time. Within two hours, every little critter is dead. Then I just go back in and air out the property and relight the pilot lights, which usually takes about a half-hour. It's quick, easy, and inexpensive. Problem solved again.

Bed bugs

Bed bugs are another more complicated issue. Bed bugs were virtually wiped out with the use of DDT, but since its use has been banned, the little buggers are making a comeback. As the world has become much more mobile, these little guys can easily go from place to place faster than they ever have before.

If you get these in your property, it is something you will need to address immediately. I have only had one case in all the years I've been in this business, but I expect it to become more of a problem in the future.

If you do get bed bugs in your property, the costs can easily escalate into the thousands of dollars. They are not easy to eradicate. Most pesticide products don't work on them. If your area is small, you can have a "treatment" done. A service will come to the house and spray the affected area where the bugs like to hide during the day. They are nocturnal and come out during the night. The cost may be a few hundred dollars to have it done. A full treatment, where the service returns several times to reapply the chemicals, may cost over a thousand dollars.

If however, your problem is extensive, then the best solution on the market right now is to have the inside temperature of your property heated to over 100 degrees. Their bodies are not hardy enough to withstand the intense heat and it kills them and their eggs.

This will be expensive, since portable heaters have to be brought inside the building for many hours to boost the heat up to the desired temperature. Let's hope that such an extreme, inconvenient, and costly remedy can be avoided.

While this measure is extreme and like anything else, is not foolproof, it is probably the best way to get rid of the problem. It is expensive and can cost thousands of dollars, so I suggest trying your more inexpensive solutions first; but make sure you address this problem immediately before it gets out of control.

Rodents/small mammals

Small animals are tricky, especially if you get squirrels inside your building. The red squirrels are the worst. It is almost impossible to get rid of them. I call them non-paying tenants and it's my job to evict them as soon as I can!! Mice, moles, etc. are far easier to catch—you just set a trap for them and you've got them in a short amount of time—but squirrels, especially red squirrels, are very smart. I've had them steal the bait out of my traps without tripping the mechanisms many times. I don't like using the small green bait that they take back to their nest since once they ingest it, they will most likely die behind the walls, in some place narrow, such as in your attic or up in a drop ceiling, etc.—and that is also something you do not want. If they die where you can't get to them easily, they can start to smell and you definitely do not want that.

I prefer live traps over kill traps; and once I catch a squirrel, I relocate it to a park several miles away. Supposedly, if you relocate them within close proximity to your property, they can find their way back to your property and you definitely don't want that either. So I err on the side of caution and move them a few miles away. It is very satisfying to catch one, see it up close, and then set it loose a few miles away! I've found that peanut butter works well, but peanuts work the best as bait. Believe me, this way works incredibly well!

CHAPTER 29
Children And Other Guests

I allow tenants to have their children and other guests stay overnight as long as they don't end up living there. That's why it's nice to be aware of what's going on at your property and make those unannounced visits from time to time. I usually only allow guests and/or children to be over a couple days a week. Children come over mostly on the weekends and many times it's every other weekend, depending on what arrangements the parents have made with each other. The children/guests are rarely allowed to stay over every weekend at the property. It just isn't fair to the other tenants. Keep in mind that if you allowed every tenant to have a guest over every day of the week, then at times you'd have 5 – 6 tenants and 5 – 6 of their guests at the property all the time!! That drives your utilities up and increases the wear and tear on your property exponentially. You want neither one of those things to happen that frequently. Usually, other tenants are good about letting you know what's going on at the house and you can inform the tenant about the increase in guests and get it quickly remedied!

CHAPTER 30
Cable And Internet

Cable

I love cable! It's relatively inexpensive, when the cost is divided among the number of people at the rental; it's also a huge "plus" when owning a rental property. Tenants love having FREE cable!! When you tell them that it's included in the rent, you've probably just found yourself a new long-term tenant!

I always love finding a house that's already wired for cable in each of the bedrooms. I think of each bedroom as its own house within a house, so each house has to have cable in it. So if it's already wired in each bedroom, then it saves me the trouble of having to install it. If the outside of the house has vinyl or steel siding, hiding holes and wires is often a problem. So if you can, try to avoid it. Otherwise, keep it to a minimum and keep it neat. It's better if you can run the wires inside, where something like a drop ceiling in the basement can hide them with ease but still make them accessible. The cable installers are very professional, so it's always best to tell them what you want and then let them do the job you've hired them to do.

In a rooming house, cable allows each tenant to watch whatever he wants, in his own private living space, his bedroom. There is no arguing among the tenants over the remote, there is no worrying as to who was supposed to have the TV on a certain night, etc. This way, each and every tenant can watch TV when they want and how they want. This is a necessity for rooming houses. I always have cable put into each bedroom, if it's not already there, and also in one or two of the common areas of the house on each level. You will have some tenants who are social, and others who are not. You'll want to cater to each variety of tenant. I've had houses where everyone stays in his or her own room practically all the time; I've also had the complete opposite, with people in the same common room socializing together all the time. I love both types of housing personalities and this is what I strive for—"housing harmony." In either case, tenants are happy and will stay longer. That, in turn, makes you happy!

Basic cable costs about $110 per month in most areas. The more competition among providers, the better deals you're likely to find. Like everything else, costs continue to rise. You want to keep an eye on competitor's prices; and if possible, switch providers if it doesn't cause a lot of headaches. I've thought about switching to satellite service from time to time; however, I have shied away from it because of its unreliability during extreme weather and because of the extra equipment involved. These plans may provide up to four receiver units, but you have to pay extra for more units and their installation fees. This can increase your costs and lead to a tenant damaging or stealing a receiver box. They are not cheap. Same goes for cable. When my local cable provider switched us over from analog boxes to digital boxes, I provided a digital box in every room; but as time went on, the costs mounted and multiplied. Then I was informed that if these boxes were damaged or stolen, it would cost me an additional $250 per box to replace! So, I made the decision to remove the boxes as each tenant moved out. Once the boxes were removed, my monthly costs were reduced and my loss exposure diminished.

Most tenants aren't that worried about the cable boxes. They are perfectly happy with the 70+ channels that basic cable packages provide. Once in a while, I do have a tenant who will want to get an HD box; when that happens, I just pass on the charges to the tenant from the cable provider. The tenant is happy to work out this kind of arrangement.

Every six months or so, you should contact your cable/satellite provider to see if they have any promotions resulting in a discount. They want your business and the cable/Internet business is very competitive—more so today than ever before, since people have many more choices than even five years ago. Now, you've not only got cable and satellite, but consumers also have Internet, cell phones, and other devices. If you have multiple properties with the same cable/satellite provider, they might be even more willing to give you a generous discount. Even if you have no intention on switching to another provider, you might play that card. It has worked successfully for me in the past.

Internet

Internet, like cable, is something I have enjoyed providing to my tenants. It has become relatively inexpensive, especially when bundled with the same service, like cable. You can get significant savings for bundling services like this and the tenant benefits from the additional service. These days, most tenants want high-speed Internet available, so if you can provide that service and make it available to all of your tenants rather inexpensively, it will attract and retain tenants for your business.

Most of the time, this cost is relativity insignificant as you can only have one modem and router per property so everyone has to use it. When you divide the cost among all the tenants, it's a minor cost with maximum benefits to your bottom line.

The only thing I do not provide is the equipment (i.e. modem, router, computers, etc.). Equipment is constantly changing and can easily be stolen or broken, so I let the tenants take care of that aspect.

CHAPTER 31
Bookkeeping

Keeping it simple is always best. There are numerous bookkeeping/accounting software packages on the market that work well for this rental property business and some will even help you generate your tax return. They are great tools to keep abreast of the cash inflows and outflows from your business. You know at any moment where you stand, cash-flow-wise. There are even apps available for your cell phone/tablet. When you're first starting your business, you may not need any fancy software or apps to make it work for you, but eventually you will want the additional help the programs offer. They can simplify your business and help you make sure you're not missing any key costs or write-offs.

As your portfolio of properties grows, you may want to have a professional bookkeeper or accountant take care of your paperwork. Once again, a bookkeeper/accountant is an invaluable person to have as part of your team.

One thing I have always found helpful is to keep very good records of all my purchases and expenses. I keep every receipt for every property. The rules keep changing on how long to keep tax returns and receipts, but the general rule of thumb is three years for personal and five to seven years for commercial/professional businesses.

I keep all my receipts so that if I need to return something a week or a few months later, I will usually have less of a problem returning that item. The item could also happen to be on sale the week I return it and I could be credited back less than the full price I paid for the item; or, the store may not even carry that particular item in stock anymore and won't return it at all with no proof that it was purchased there.

Another reason why it is important to keep all your receipts and to keep good records of all your purchases and expenses is because this is where some of your most significant tax write-offs occur for your business—and having detailed records are vital in proving that your purchase or expense for the business actually took place. You don't want to be worried about being audited, but you also want to have the proof in case you are—and you will have that proof as long as you maintain and keep detailed records of your expenses and purchases for your business. Contact your bookkeeper or accountant as your business gets more complicated.

CHAPTER 32
Washers/Dryers

Providing washing machines and dryers is a great draw to attract and keep tenants at your properties. This added service is very valuable to tenants. I have always included washing machines and dryers that are not coin-operated at my properties. If you wanted to make them coin-operated, it would provide an ideal source of extra income. You can program them to charge whatever amount you want. I would suggest making them slightly less expensive than area laundromats. Be sure to check them regularly so that no one breaks into the machines and steals any profit from you.

I haven't installed coin-op machines, specifically because of their up-front cost. They are significantly more expensive (two-to-three-times as much) than non-coin-op machines. Over time, depending on how many loads of laundry are done at the property, you may recoup this cost.

CHAPTER 33
Vending Machines

You could also have vending machines at the property. I have considered having soda machines and other vending machines on the properties for the additional revenue, but have not pursued the thought. In my opinion, they are just one more thing that has to be maintained regularly and restocked daily or weekly, not to mention the power usage they pull. A refrigerated unit like a pop machine would draw a large amount of electricity and subtract from your bottom line.

CHAPTER 34
Ice Dams And Their Removal

It doesn't sound like a serious thing, but given enough time or enough snow from a few big snowstorms, ice dams can become very serious. If you're in an area where you don't often get large quantities of snow, then you can skip over this section, but if you do, read below.

Ice dams are caused by the warmer air inside your house rising up into a poorly-insulated attic area, which causes the snow on the roof to melt.

The warmer melting snow slides down the shingles and freezes just above the eaves. For example, when the water goes out beyond the edges of the attic on overhangs and soffits, it cools and freezes. This thaw-freeze can continue until huge ice ridges form. Once the ice ridges form, additional melt water above the ice ridges will creep under the shingles and leak into the house. This will result in major interior damage.

The best way to avoid this is to get your attic properly insulated and any "pass-throughs," that can lead all the way from the basement up to the attic, sealed up. There is a significant upfront expense, but believe me: it will save you lots of time and money later on. Make sure your attic vents are open and there is good airflow. This keeps your attic cool in the winter, helping to prevent ice dams.

Sometimes, though, you won't know if your roof has a problem with ice dams until it does snow. You can usually tell within a day or two after a large snowstorm if you're going to have a problem. Within that time frame, icicles will start to form. The larger they are and the more frequent, the more of a problem you could potentially have.

When this happens, you need to address it as soon as you can. There are a few options you can try that I have used.

First, the cheapest way is to get a roof rake and "rake" the snow off the roof. This is similar to a shovel, only the scoop part faces backwards towards you. There are a number of long aluminum pole pieces that attach to it for reaching various heights. This is usually done from the ground. You just attach the pieces together and lift it up in the air and onto the roof and reach up the roofline as far as you can, and pull it towards you. As you're pulling the rake towards you, the rake slides down the roof and the snow is removed. You're not hurting your shingles either since you're pulling down the roof in the same direction they're layered one on top of the other. You can buy a good roof rake for about $20 – $30. I have had one for years and it's lasted me a good long time. Raking roof snow myself has saved me a lot of time and money over the years too.

NOTE: Always be aware of where your power lines are when doing this! The pole ends may be plastic and rubber tipped, but you are still dealing with a large metal object that you are "waving" in the air!

Second, you can get electric "heat cables" and put them up on the roof. They easily remove ice dams. Install them in the warmer months. If you haven't had time to mount them on the roof, you can drape them over the ice dams and within a couple of days they will melt through the area you intended. You will have to come back and move them around to the other sections of the roof and sometimes they will get frozen into sections of the ice dam as they are melting it. This of course makes it harder to move them around, but it also helps to keep them from sliding off the roof. Heat cables work best once they are mounted on the roof. Installation is easy, and costs only $15 – $20 for about 50 feet of cable. They do pull enough wattage to be noticeable on your electric bill, so be mindful of this additional expense.

The third, most difficult, and possibly expensive option is to just get up on the roof and shovel. If you do it yourself, it is back-breaking work and very dangerous! So be careful if you choose this method.

Having someone else come to clear your roof for you may be a better option. I've had entire roofs cleaned and steamed off for as little as $400. There are companies available who remove just the snow from the roof and/or the ice dams as well. The more difficult and/or dangerous the work, of course the more expensive it will be. Again, it just depends on your maintenance budget. If you're just starting out, then you may want to do it yourself; if you've been at this a while, your time is more important. If your cash flow is fine, then definitely have someone else do it for you.

CHAPTER 35
Collecting Rent

Rent drawer

My tenants put their monthly rent payments in the "rent drawer." Some landlords prefer to have rent mailed to them and still others will have their tenants deposit payments into a bank account set up for that purpose.

I choose to have the rent drawer for the simple reason that it gives me an opportunity to come inside the property each month and see how things are going. You also have the opportunity to speak with your tenants on a regular basis and to pass on any valuable information to them. They have the opportunity to bring up any issues or concerns, or just have a friendly chat. Again, I recommend visiting your properties at least once a month to keep an eye on things. Get used to being a proactive business owner.

Tenants like the convenience of a "rent drawer"; I like it since I don't have to go knocking on doors to collect the rent. I visit the property on the 6th of the month and if a tenant's rent isn't in the drawer, then it's late. My lease allows tenants until the 5th of the month to pay their rent on time.

I tape a nice simple nametag to the outside of the drawer so that everyone knows its purpose, a sample of which is in Appendix E. Feel free to use it for your business.

I do have tenants who prefer to mail their rent to me and many who allow me to enter their rooms each month when they have their rent ready for me. All options work well and none of them are wrong. You can pick and choose which ones works for your style and your business.

CHAPTER 36
Insurance

Not only are you required to pay for hazard insurance to cover your mortgage on a monthly basis, but you also will have to pay for annual property insurance for such things as a catastrophic event (tornado, fire, etc.) or in the event a tenant slips and falls at one of your properties.

Umbrella policy

An additional option you should consider as an extra level of insurance is what's called an "umbrella policy." It is a type of insurance that goes above and beyond what property insurance covers and has higher limits. In the unfortunate event you were to get sued by a tenant or a repair person, the umbrella policy kicks in to help decrease the likelihood that you will lose everything you've worked so hard to build. You can get a $1 million policy for about $500 a year. This is one of the most valuable pieces of insurance you can get for any business. I consider it a necessity, not an option!

Flooding

Remember, not all insurance policies are created equal. Some homeowner's and landlord's insurance policies include a section on flood damage to your property and are required by the state to be included in the policy; other states don't require this to be included as part of the regular policy. If this is not included in your policy, you will need to purchase a rider to the policy. This is important! Any change you make to your insurance takes one month for it to be considered active. So don't wait until you have damage to get this rider as part of your coverage. Be proactive and include it to begin with. Even if you think you don't live in an area that has ever been flooded, it can still happen. As is the case with many policies, your property won't be covered if the main drain or sewer line backs up and floods your basement! Most polices only cover flooding if it comes from outside and flows into the property.

If your state doesn't require this as part of the property insurance, adding a rider specifically for flooding will help save you significant time, money, and headaches in the future.

CHAPTER 37
Incorporating

There are a few choices when it comes to incorporating your business. Which one to choose? Should I incorporate or not? It can be confusing.

Primarily, you are choosing to incorporate for the tax benefits and the possible reduction to the risk of being cleaned out in a lawsuit. While helpful in both cases, they don't always provide enough benefit and safety. Incorporating may not shelter you completely. The same thing applies to your taxes. Incorporating may save you money on taxes, but you probably will still owe something.

In both cases, it's prudent to seek professional advice from your accountant and/or a lawyer who specializes in small business. You'll need to know if you should be incorporated as a sole proprietary, S corporation, C corp, or LLC. Everyone's situation is different and I know people who have chosen to incorporate their businesses in each of these types, even though their businesses were similar.

One thing to keep in mind is that in most states, if you purchase a property using funds from a mortgage company based on your personal credit and your name and not that of a corporation, the property will have to be titled in your name, as a sole proprietary, not as an S corporation or an LLC. If, however, you purchased the property with all cash, then you can incorporate it however you so choose.

Once the mortgage has been repaid, you can then re-title the property out of your name and into your company's name.

As an added layer of protection, you can manage your properties through your own management company which can be an S corporation, C corp, or an LLC. Your tenants are then doing business with the corporate entity, and not directly with you. Be sure to consult a knowledgeable small business attorney when starting your business and as your business grows. Deciding to incorporate involves state and federal tax codes, which can be extremely complex. You'll need the help of competent professionals.

CHAPTER 38
What Happens After You've Purchased Your 4th Property And Want To Purchase More

This is where you can start to run into problems financing additional properties. You'll usually have no problem getting pre-approved financing up to this point, but banks have limits on the number of loans they are willing to lend to a sole proprietor, which is at about four. If you've set up your business under your name, you will run into this problem; but if you set it up under a corporation, the loans will be backed by your business credit and not as much by your personal credit, hence a sole proprietor.

Most people, when starting out purchasing one property at a time, aren't going to be able to get the loans they need to finance properties unless they do it with their own name and their own credit.

As long as you have copies of all your leases with each tenant to show to the bank, and you have at least a few years' tax return statements, they will be willing to loan money to you to purchase your next investment. If they can't or won't, then it's time to switch to another lender. Lenders are everywhere—and where one won't find a loan that fits your needs, another will. You just have to keep looking. Don't stop looking just because one lender or broker says it can't be done or they have no clue how to get it done. I'm living proof that it can be done since I have done this repeatedly! If they're going to be negative or can't get you qualified for a loan, you don't want them on your team anyways.

One of the best ways to do this is to use a mortgage broker. They aren't obligated to use just the loans that one bank offers; they deal with multiple banks, financial institutions, and even private lenders. Each bank, financial institution, or private lender may have four or five loans—and together that can be a pool of dozens to hundreds of types of loan packages.

I have dealt with many different mortgage brokers over the years and they have most always been able to find a loan that works for my situation at the time.

If you are denied repeatedly, after your fourth property, it is a good time to look at what is going on. If you haven't done so already, ask the lender what you can do to get approved.

You may also want to look at your credit report. Once you are denied credit, you can get a copy of your credit report for free.

CHAPTER 39
Designated As "Primary Residence"

Another option that can make it easier to get financing on additional properties is to make the purchase of your new property your primary residence. It is usually easier to get financing if it's for your primary residence.

Here's how it usually works. You purchase your fist property, move into it, and start renting it out. After a couple of years of living there, renting it, building your down payment fund and your credit, you decide it's time to purchase your next property. You've looked into the financing of non-homeowner occupied loans, or investment property loans as they're also called, and you find out that the mortgage payment is a few hundred dollars more a month since it's considered an investment property and not your primary residence.

There's a mortgage rule called "New Every Two" which qualifies borrowers as a "new" homeowner every two years even if you're not an actual "new" homeowner. This means that as long as you purchase a property and it's been at least two years since your last purchase and you designate it your primary residence, you can qualify for the lower home-owner mortgage rates, which can be as much as 1 – 2% less on a mortgage. Depending on the size of the mortgage, this is very significant indeed!

So, if you don't mind moving to and living in your new property every two years, you can qualify for the home-owner occupied lower mortgage rates on each additional purchase. If, however, you choose not to or can't move there, then you will have to purchase the property at the investor or non-homeowner occupied rates.

One thing to remember is that if you do move from one property to another, and your original property was your primary residence, and you then designate your new purchase as your primary residence, you'll want to contact the city or county you live in to change the primary residence designation to your new address. You can't have more than one property designated as your primary residence. Your primary residence usually qualifies you for a property tax discount compared to non-primary residences and it is not allowed by law to get this tax break on more than one property at a time.

CHAPTER 40
Other Benefits

Providing a needed service to your community!

Of course you are in this business to make money, but you are also providing a much-needed service to your community. There are many people who need housing like this and literally have nowhere else to go. I have had many people, over the years, thank me for providing this service; I've had many other people who have stayed with me for a while, moved out, and come back to me years later when they need this type of rental again. Once you have been in this business long enough, you will start to get repeat tenants and referrals from past tenants. Those are some of my best tenants. I know them and they know me—and I'm usually more willing to rent to them again. This is much better than a reference, since we have done business together before. Because I have proven to them that I am professional and fair, they often return to rent again.

Tax write-offs

This is another subject I'll just touch on briefly. Tax write-offs can be significant when it comes to rental property. The tax laws vary greatly if you "actively" manage and maintain the properties yourself versus having a management company "passively" do the work for you. As with any tax issue(s), consult your tax professional regarding the write-offs available to you. Every state and county has different rules. In this case, your accountant/bookkeeper, one of the many valuable people on your team, will know the things you can and cannot write-off and how it pertains to your individual situation.

Tenants' former possessions

People will be people. Intentionally or not, they leave things behind. Over the years I have accumulated a vast amount of items from former tenants. Of course, much of it is not worth anything, but there are many treasures left behind as well. Once you have done your best to contact the former tenant and waited the designated period of time required by the laws of your city, state, or county, which will dictate how you hold and store former tenant's possessions, they are then yours to do with whatever you wish. After this holding period is over, I have either discarded the items, kept them for my own use, or sold them on sites like CL or eBay. You name it, it gets left behind. I've inherited expensive jewelry, high-end furniture, top-of-the-line tools, trailers, building materials, etc., etc. If I ever failed as a landlord, I could get into the used furniture business. I'd call it Bob's Used Furniture Barn for all the furniture I've inherited. Once in a while, selling "left-behind" stuff will give you some handy *pocket money*.

Building lasting relationships

I try not to get too friendly with my tenants, since some tenants will try to take advantage of the relationship. It's always best to keep a little space between yourself and your tenants; but you'll find that over time, you may be able to build long lasting friendships with some tenants. I've rented to people from all walks of life, from all over the world. You learn from them, and they from you. Since they know you, they are also a very good source of referrals.

Coupons/deals

Whenever I visit my properties I try to do as many things as possible, so whatever else I'm doing I also look at the pile of mail that arrives daily at my properties that invariably stacks up. Most of the mail is for current tenants; there is also a large amount of mail for former tenants. I mark them "return to sender" and put them in the mail the next time I'm at the post office. Mixed in with all this mail are large amounts of junk mail. I am always looking for deals, coupons, and bargains—not only for my business, but also for meals, entertainment, travel, etc. Since my properties are close together, they often get the same coupons mailed to them. This is an overlooked bonus that you can use. For example, there may be a coupon to one of your favorite restaurants that gets mailed to each of your properties. I collect these coupons and use them. Now I have multiple coupons for my favorite restaurants. This may not be a big deal to many people, but I love to go out to eat and I like to keep my expenses at a minimum. A deal is a deal, no matter where it comes from—and multiples of the same deal are even better!

These are free, culled from junk mail. Use and enjoy them, give them away, sell them ... you choose.

Skills learned

There are numerous skills I've acquired over the years. There are two things I've never wanted to do as part of my career: give speeches and make sales calls. Sales and speeches weren't my strong suit growing up. Many years later, reflecting on that list, I realize that I do those very things every day. I now do small speeches when I'm talking with a group of tenants, or I'm selling my property to a potential tenant who I'm trying to convince to move in. So I literally do give speeches and make sales calls on a regular basis, they're just not door to door. The ironies of life! LOL.

Along with that, I've improved my skill set in many areas. I've become very knowledgeable at basic accounting, lawn care, plumbing, HVAC, wiring, electrical, managing/bargaining with repair and service technicians, time management, finance, patience, and all the trade skills involved with building, repairing, and maintaining a single family home (roofing, siding, flooring, interior and exterior finishing, egress windows, wiring, retaining walls, driveway finishes, etc.). The list of valuable skills goes on and on.

A real-world education, your real estate PhD!

With this business I've gained a wealth of knowledge and skills that I couldn't get without the real-world experience of running my own business and building it from scratch. I've effectively earned a *real-world PhD* in business, one house at a time! It's important to note that my tenants have paid me to get this incredible, hands-on education!!

CHAPTER 41
Exit Strategy

Each person's going to have different goals, so therefore everyone will have their own "exit strategy." There is no right or wrong here. It is entirely dependent on what your ultimate objective is. Do you want to start with something small and work into larger properties/investments and then sell out within 5 – 10 years, or do you plan on keeping them long-term and using them to faze yourself out of your job?

The best part is, you're not locked into any one choice. Your exit strategy can change as you age, or as your needs change. What you want today is not necessarily what you'll want tomorrow. In the end, the decision is yours and you have several choices. There are many options.

In the interest of helping you out, I will share with you my exit strategy—not as what you should do, but just as an example of what can be done.

I have always been a *buy-and-hold* type of investor. All of my investments have been held this way. I'm not in this for the quick flip or short-term rental; I'm in this for the long term: ten, twenty, and even thirty years of holding a single piece of property. So my exit strategy is to keep them long term, pay them off, and then use the income to pay for my retirement years.

It just depends on the deal and what tomorrow brings. Over the past decade, I've been perfectly content with buying these properties and holding them long term. If you buy them right, so they cash flow well, you'll never have to sell and the choice will always be yours to make.

You have the interest, now jump in. It's simple. Learn from it. Grow with it. We alone limit ourselves.

I wish you the best!

APPENDIX A
Copy Of Lease

APPENDIX A - Copy of Lease

RENTAL AGREEMENT

THIS AGREEMENT EXISTS BETWEEN____ (your company name), LANDLORD OF _____, AND THE UNDERSIGNED TENANT.

THE TENANT AGREES TO RENT ONE BEDROOM AT _____ FROM THE LANDLORD AT THE MONTHLY RENT OF $_____. THIS DOES NOT INCLUDE GARAGE. THIS AGREEMENT IS ON A MONTH TO MONTH BASIS. THE LANDLORD OR TENANT MAY END THIS AGREEMENT WITH ONE FULL CALENDAR MONTH'S NOTICE, (CALENDAR MONTH IS FROM THE 1ST TO THE END OF THE MONTH.) TENANT IS RESPONSIBLE FOR RENT FOR ONE FULL CALENDAR MONTH AFTER WRITTEN NOTICE HAS BEEN GIVEN. RENT INCLUDES ALL NORMAL UTILITIES – ELECTRICITY, GAS, WATER, GARBAGE AND CABLE TV. YOU MAY INSTALL YOUR OWN PRIVATE LINE AT YOUR OWN EXPENSE.

THE TENANT AGREES TO PAY RENT IN FULL ON THE FIRST DAY OF THE MONTH. IF RENT IS NOT PAID IN FULL BY THE 5th OF THE MONTH, A $50.00 LATE FEE WILL BE CHARGED TO THE TENANT AND YOU WILL BE GIVEN ONE CALENDAR MONTH'S NOTICE TO MOVE OUT. IF THE RENT IS NOT PAID IN FULL BY THE 10th OF THE MONTH AN ADDITIONAL $50.00 LATE FEE WILL BE CHARGED. IF RENT IS PAID IN FULL, THEN ONE MONTH'S NOTICE IS RESCINDED. ALL BOUNCE CHECK FEES CHARGED BY THE BANKS WILL ALSO BE PASSED ON TO THE TENANT IN THE AMOUNT OF $25.00, OR HIGHER IF THE BANK FEES ARE HIGHER. RENT PAYMENTS CAN BE LEFT IN THE RENT DRAWER OR MAILED TO (your company name and address). THE OFFICE TELEPHONE IS (__) ___-___. ONLY ONE TENANT IS ALLOWED PER BEDROOM. NO PETS ARE ALLOWED. NO SMOKING IS ALLOWED INSIDE THE BUILDING. ONLY ONE CAR PER TENANT IS ALLOWED. ILLEGAL DRUGS USED OR SOLD IN ANY SHAPE OR FORM IS GROUNDS FOR IMMEDIATE EVICTION. PROSTITUTION IS ALSO GROUNDS FOR IMMEDIATE EVICTION. LANDLORD RESERVES THE RIGHT UNDER STATE LAW TO INSPECT THE PROPERTY AND PREMISES AT ANY TIME.

RESPONSIBILITY – TENANT IS EXPECTED TO CLEAN UP AFTER THEMSELVES AND HELP KEEP COMMON AREAS OF THE HOUSE CLEAN. TENANTS MAY NOT USE OTHER PEOPLE'S PROPERTY WITHOUT PERMISSION. TENANTS ARE EXPECTED TO TURN OFF UNUSED LIGHTS AND MUST PAY EXTRA IF THEY WASTE UTILITIES. DO NOT LEAVE PERSONAL ITEMS STREWN ABOUT AND RETURN ITEMS AFTER THEY ARE USED. TENANT IS RESPONSIBLE FOR ANY DAMAGE DONE TO THE HOUSE OR CONTENTS BY THEMSELVES OR THEIR GUESTS. IT IS THE TENANT'S RESPONSIBILITY TO HAVE RENTER'S INSURANCE FOR ANY PERSONAL ITEMS.

ATTITUDE – IN ORDER FOR PEOPLE TO LIVE TOGETHER UNDER THE SAME ROOF, COOPERATION AND ATTITUDE ARE IMPORTANT. COMMUNICATION IS ENCOURAGED SO THAT EVERYONE CAN ENJOY LIVING HERE. I AM SEEKING TENANTS WHO ARE MATURE, RESPONSIBLE, COOPERATIVE, PROFESSIONAL, AND HAVE A POSITIVE ATTITUDE. IF TENANT OR LANDLORD ARE UNHAPPY WITH THE RELATIONSHIP, ONLY A FULL CALENDAR MONTH'S NOTICE IS NEEDED BY EITHER AND THERE ARE NO HARD FEELINGS.

INCENTIVE – AS LONG AS TENANT MAINTAINS CONTINUOUS OCCUPANCY, THE LANDLORD AGREES TO NEVER RAISE THE RENT. THE LANDLORD ALSO AGREES THAT ALL NORMAL UTILITIES WILL ALWAYS BE INCLUDED IN THE RENT.

DEPOSITS EQUAL TO ONE CALENDAR MONTH'S RENT IS COLLECTED. ALL MONEY RECEIVED FOR RENT IS NON-REFUNDABLE. DEPOSIT IS NON-REFUNDABLE IF ANY CONDITIONS OF AGREEMENT ARE BROKEN. PER MINNESOTA STATE LAW, LANDLORD HAS 21 DAYS INTO FOLLOWING MONTH TO RETURN DEPOSITS.

THIS AGREEMENT IS ENTERED INTO ON _____. OCCUPANCY STARTS _____

RENT AMOUNT PAID _____, NON-REFUNDABLE, FOR _____

DEPOSIT AMOUNT PAID. _____.

LANDLORD   I AGREE TO THE ABOVE TERMS (signature of tenant)   TENANT (print tenant's name)

VEHICLE MAKE & MODEL   VEHICLE PLATE #   EMPLOYER

SOCIAL SECURITY NUMBER   EMERGENCY CONTACT

APPENDIX B
Property Information

APPENDIX B - Property Information

Helpful information for the tenants to remember. Post it in a visible spot at the property, such as on the refrigerator.

The address here is:

(street address)
(city, state, zip)

Garbage day is:

Every _(enter day here)_ morning, unless there is a holiday earlier in the week, then it will be the following day.

For any repairs that need to be made on the house, please call:

name at: *651-123-4567*

If questions, or in case of emergency **(owner/manager)** *can be reached at:*

(612) 123-4567

APPENDIX C
Eviction Notice

APPENDIX C - Eviction Notice

EVICTION NOTICE

_____, this is to notify you that as of today, the _____ of _____, your rent is now past due. Since I have not heard from you and you have not paid your rent, this is your one month's notice to move out of my property, your place of residence at _____. Please have all of your things removed by from the property by the end of the month, if not sooner.

Please note that if your rent, in the amount of $_____ plus all late fees, is brought up to date and paid by the 15th of the month, this notice is null and void.

Thank you.

(owner/manager name)
(company name)

EVICTION NOTICE

_____, this is to notify you that as of today, the _____ of _____, your rent is now past due. Since I have not heard from you and you have not paid your rent, this is your one month's notice to move out of my property, your place of residence at _____. Please have all of your things removed by from the property by the end of the month, if not sooner.

Please note that if your rent, in the amount of $_____ plus all late fees, is brought up to date and paid by the 15th of the month, this notice is null and void.

Thank you.

(owner/manager name)
(company name)

EVICTION NOTICE

_____, this is to notify you that as of today, the _____ of _____, your rent is now past due. Since I have not heard from you and you have not paid your rent, this is your one month's notice to move out of my property, your place of residence at _____. Please have all of your things removed by from the property by the end of the month, if not sooner.

Please note that if your rent, in the amount of $_____ plus all late fees, is brought up to date and paid by the 15th of the month, this notice is null and void.

Thank you.

(owner/manager name)
(company name)

APPENDIX D
Reminders

APPENDIX D - Reminders
(Copy and cut out for placement on washer/dryer or sink(s))

Please be considerate of the other tenants and limit *YOUR* usage of the washer and dryer to:

9am – 9pm

Thank you,
Management

Please clean out the Lint Trap after each use.

Please DO NOT leave dirty dishes in or around the sink. Put them in the dishwasher.

Please be considerate of the other tenants and limit *YOUR* usage of the washer and dryer to:

9am – 9pm

Thank you,
Management

Please clean out the Lint Trap after each use.

Please DO NOT leave dirty dishes in or around the sink. Put them in the dishwasher.

APPENDIX E
Rent Drawer

APPENDIX E - Rent Drawer

RENT DRAWER

APPENDIX F
Thermostat Settings

APPENDIX F - Thermostat Settings

Please keep the temperature between 70 – 75 degrees Fahrenheit at all times. DO NOT adjust this temperature outside this range.

Please keep the temperature between 70 – 75 degrees Fahrenheit at all times. DO NOT adjust this temperature outside this range.

Please keep the temperature between 70 – 75 degrees Fahrenheit at all times. DO NOT adjust this temperature outside this range.

Please keep the temperature between 70 – 75 degrees Fahrenheit at all times. DO NOT adjust this temperature outside this range.

Please keep the temperature between 70 – 75 degrees Fahrenheit at all times. DO NOT adjust this temperature outside this range.

APPENDIX G
Duct Cleaning

APPENDIX G - Duct Cleaning
(example of what you can say...)

DUCT CLEANING

Everyone,

I am having the ductwork in the house cleaned out. This is to help reduce dust and allergen particles in the air, thereby making it a "healthier" house to live in and to help the A/C run more efficiently.

Since the duct cleaners will need access to every duct and vent in the house to properly clean them, please have the vents in your room free from anything blocking them. I will be letting them into each and every room to access these vents. You do not need to leave during this process, but please know that the driveway will be blocked for a few hours, so plan accordingly.

They will be here on **Wednesday, June 30th** between **11:00am and Noon** for about 2-3 hours. Thank you for your help.

Management

DUCT CLEANING

Everyone,

I am having the ductwork in the house cleaned out. This is to help reduce dust and allergen particles in the air, thereby making it a "healthier" house to live in and to help the A/C run more efficiently.

Since the duct cleaners will need access to every duct and vent in the house to properly clean them, please have the vents in your room free from anything blocking them. I will be letting them into each and every room to access these vents. You do not need to leave during this process, but please know that the driveway will be blocked for a few hours, so plan accordingly.

They will be here on **Wednesday, June 30th** between **11:00am and Noon** for about 2-3 hours. Thank you for your help.

Management

DUCT CLEANING

Everyone,

I am having the ductwork in the house cleaned out. This is to help reduce dust and allergen particles in the air, thereby making it a "healthier" house to live in and to help the A/C run more efficiently.

Since the duct cleaners will need access to every duct and vent in the house to properly clean them, please have the vents in your room free from anything blocking them. I will be letting them into each and every room to access these vents. You do not need to leave during this process, but please know that the driveway will be blocked for a few hours, so plan accordingly.

They will be here on **Wednesday, June 30th** between **11:00am and Noon** for about 2-3 hours. Thank you for your help.

Management

APPENDIX H
Front Door Lock Change

APPENDIX H - Front Door Lock Change

On Sunday, January 10th at 12:30pm I will be changing the locks on the house. Please be available to exchange your keys for new keys. This pertains to the front door only.

Thank you.

Management

On Sunday, January 10th at 12:30pm I will be changing the locks on the house. Please be available to exchange your keys for new keys. This pertains to the front door only.

Thank you.

Management

On Sunday, January 10th at 12:30pm I will be changing the locks on the house. Please be available to exchange your keys for new keys. This pertains to the front door only.

Thank you.

Management

APPENDIX I
Carpet Cleaning

APPENDIX I - Carpet Cleaning

CARPET CLEANING

Everyone,

Tomorrow, Wednesday, **August 13, 2008** the carpet cleaners will be here around **1:00pm**. I will be having most of the carpet in the house cleaned. Please make sure you remove your shoes from now on. The carpet will take 48-72 hours to dry. During that time, you may want to have a pair of "inside" shoes to wear around the house and a separate pair to wear outside. Please be careful when walking from the carpet to the linoleum. It is very easy to slip on these surfaces once the carpet has been cleaned.

Thank you for your help. Management

CARPET CLEANING

Everyone,

Tomorrow, Wednesday, **August 13, 2008** the carpet cleaners will be here around **1:00pm**. I will be having most of the carpet in the house cleaned. Please make sure you remove your shoes from now on. The carpet will take 48-72 hours to dry. During that time, you may want to have a pair of "inside" shoes to wear around the house and a separate pair to wear outside. Please be careful when walking from the carpet to the linoleum. It is very easy to slip on these surfaces once the carpet has been cleaned.

Thank you for your help. Management

CARPET CLEANING

Everyone,

Tomorrow, Wednesday, **August 13, 2008** the carpet cleaners will be here around **1:00pm**. I will be having most of the carpet in the house cleaned. Please make sure you remove your shoes from now on. The carpet will take 48-72 hours to dry. During that time, you may want to have a pair of "inside" shoes to wear around the house and a separate pair to wear outside. Please be careful when walking from the carpet to the linoleum. It is very easy to slip on these surfaces once the carpet has been cleaned.

Thank you for your help. Management

CARPET CLEANING

Everyone,

Tomorrow, Wednesday, **August 13, 2008** the carpet cleaners will be here around **1:00pm**. I will be having most of the carpet in the house cleaned. Please make sure you remove your shoes from now on. The carpet will take 48-72 hours to dry. During that time, you may want to have a pair of "inside" shoes to wear around the house and a separate pair to wear outside. Please be careful when walking from the carpet to the linoleum. It is very easy to slip on these surfaces once the carpet has been cleaned.

Thank you for your help. Management

APPENDIX J

De-Bugging House

APPENDIX J - De-Bugging House

DE-BUGGING HOUSE

Everyone,

Its that time of year again. Spring is in the air and the insects are coming out of hiding. I will be de-bugging the house on **Sunday, May 6th at 12pm (Noon) till 2pm**. This will involve using fogging cans that will kill all types of insects in the house, even insects that are hidden behind walls. Please cover any food you have in your rooms, cover sensitive electronics and shut off any fans/heaters you may have. Please make sure your windows are closed.

This will take at least 1 hour to work and then another 1 hour to air out the house. Please **DO NOT ENTER** the house during this time. Everyone must be outside. I will be here to watch the house so you can leave your rooms open if you choose. (You will see better results if your rooms are left open).

Thank you. Management

Everyone,

Its that time of year again. Spring is in the air and the insects are coming out of hiding. I will be de-bugging the house on **Sunday, May 6th at 12pm (Noon) till 2pm**. This will involve using fogging cans that will kill all types of insects in the house, even insects that are hidden behind walls. Please cover any food you have in your rooms, cover sensitive electronics and shut off any fans/heaters you may have. Please make sure your windows are closed.

This will take at least 1 hour to work and then another 1 hour to air out the house. Please **DO NOT ENTER** the house during this time. Everyone must be outside. I will be here to watch the house so you can leave your rooms open if you choose. (You will see better results if your rooms are left open).

Thank you. Management

Everyone,

Its that time of year again. Spring is in the air and the insects are coming out of hiding. I will be de-bugging the house on **Sunday, May 6th at 12pm (Noon) till 2pm**. This will involve using fogging cans that will kill all types of insects in the house, even insects that are hidden behind walls. Please cover any food you have in your rooms, cover sensitive electronics and shut off any fans/heaters you may have. Please make sure your windows are closed.

This will take at least 1 hour to work and then another 1 hour to air out the house. Please **DO NOT ENTER** the house during this time. Everyone must be outside. I will be here to watch the house so you can leave your rooms open if you choose. (You will see better results if your rooms are left open).

Thank you. Management

ABOUT THE AUTHOR

Robert W. Rutledge has been involved with the rooming house business, both as a tenant and an owner, for over 24 years. The success of his rooming house business has allowed him to branch off into other types of real estate and he has since diversified his portfolio into larger properties. He currently resides with his family in Minnesota and is contemplating an early retirement. He loves watching football and enjoys mountain biking and martial arts. He is also pursuing a number of ideas to be patented and rolled out in the years ahead.